GEN**X**PAT

GENXPAT

The Young Professional's Guide to Making a Successful Life Abroad

Margaret Malewski

INTERCULTURAL PRESS
A Nicholas Brealey Publishing Company

YARMOUTH, ME • BOSTON • LONDON

First published by Intercultural Press, a Nicholas Brealey Publishing Company, in 2005.

Intercultural Press, Inc., a Nicholas Brealey Publishing Company
PO Box 700, Yarmouth, Maine 04096 USA
Information: 1-888-BREALEY
Orders: 207-846-5168   Fax: 207-846-5181
www.interculturalpress.com

Nicholas Brealey Publishing
3-5 Spafield Street, Clerkenwell, London, EC1R 4QB, UK
Tel: +44-(0)-207-239-0360   Fax: +44-(0)-207-239-0370
www.nbrealey-books.com

Cover and text design by Lisa Garbutt

Printed in the United States of America

09   08   07   06   05   1   2   3   4   5

ISBN: 1-931930-23-6

Library of Congress Cataloging-in-Publication Data

Malewski, Margaret.
     GenXpat : the young professional 's guide to making a successful life
abroad / Margaret Malewski.
          p. cm.
     Includes bibliographical references and index.
     ISBN 1-931930-23-6
     1. Employees--Relocation.   2. Employment in foreign countries.
3. International business enterprises--Employees--Relocation.
4. Americans--Foreign countries.   I. Title.
HF5549.5.R47M345 2005
650.1—dc22

2005007808

TO CAROLINE,
for seventeen years of friendship across four continents,
and for being there at every step of the way.

CONTENTS

ACKNOWLEDGMENTS

I would like to extend my warmest thanks to the following people, without whom this book would not have been possible:

For getting me started on the GenXpat experience, being an inspiration and a mentor: Jim Lafferty, Vice President, Procter & Gamble.

For helping me find my career interest and personal balance: Michael Reddy and Jim Hayhurst at The Right Mountain, *www.therightmountain.com*.

For showing me the enjoyment of writing: Mr. Robert Hamilton, at The Study School.

For their friendship and support: Pini and Renée Abcassis, Fawaz Al Matrouk, Eric Fattah, Leyla Pardo-Figueroa and Chris Brodie, Alex Kuilman, Mylène Robic, and Christian Wernstedt.

For their love and support: my parents, Wanda and Ryszard Malewski; my sister, Anna Malewska-Szalygin; and the Guay family.

For sharing their personal stories and the insights that shaped this book: Anna Borzymowska, Guy Brusselmans, Jennifer Hamm, Zeina Hatem, Nick Kosick, Asaph Na'aman, Jesse Nobbs-Thiessen, Ulla Raithel, Paddi Rice, and Dor and Lital Sela.

For their broadening comments and perspective: Atsuko Fukuda, Elodie Richard, Glenda Davis, Hugo Vega Jímenez, Ilham Sebti-Benani, Ines Scharnweber, Jose Arce Varga, Michael Heilig, Miguel Alfaro Cuevas, and Silke Brabander.

For sharing her expertise based on 17 years in the relocation industry: Jennifer White, Global Client Services Director, Primacy Relocation.

For introducing me to the world of expat writing: Robin Pascoe, *www.expatexpert.com*.

Last, but certainly not least, I would like to acknowledge the great work of the team at Intercultural Press. Erika Heilman patiently coached me through the editorial process, offering constructive feedback, helpful suggestions, and encouragement. I would also like to thank Rebecca Greenberg for her thorough copy edit and Carmen Mitchell for her work on the promotion of the book.

INTRODUCTION

It all began when I called Jim, Marketing Director of Procter & Gamble Poland, for help with a translation. He had recruited me to join the company in Warsaw a few months before, when I still had a year to go before graduating from university, and we continued to touch base periodically. That day I had a question about the expat neighborhood he lived in and, I felt, this would be a good opportunity for us to catch up.

He sounded distracted as he answered the phone. He told me that he had a new assignment as head of the Near East business, based in Geneva, and he was about to leave for the airport. I felt my heart sink. I had really wanted to work for Jim because he had an entrepreneurial attitude that I found inspiring, and now he would no longer be based in the Warsaw office. Before I even knew it, the words spilled out, "Is there any chance I can move with you?"

I was only half-joking. I had been in Poland for six years by then, since 1992. To my Canadian eyes, it had been a fascinating experience to see a country metamorphose from a former satellite of the Soviet Union to a free-market state. Yet no matter how open the country was becoming, my Western values and upbringing still clashed with the more traditional outlook of my peers. I wasn't ready to get married and have kids, like many of the girls I knew. I wanted a career and adventure. That's why I had been looking for jobs with multinationals, preferably with the opportunity to travel outside of Poland. In this context, working for Jim in Geneva would be a dream come true.

Amazingly, Jim paused to consider my idea and promised to inquire whether I could join his new team. A few days later, the phone rang. Jim had just finished his meetings in Switzerland and was on the way to Beirut for his first market visit. He had news for me: the vice president had given his okay—there was a spot for me on the Lebanese business team, but I needed to make my decision by the end of the week... When he hung up, I headed straight for my world atlas. Where the hell was Lebanon? All I knew about the country was what I remembered seeing on CNN in the early 1990s. My mental image was of white concrete buildings with gaping holes in their sides, rubble in the streets, and soldiers in desert camouflage. Would I be working in a war zone? Was it worth staking my life for adventure and career?

Then I got an e-mail from Jim. He was, he wrote, on the roof of the Beirut Marriott Hotel, sipping a drink by the side of the pool. The sun was sinking into the blue waters of the Mediterranean Sea. The *previous evening he had gone out to dinner with the distributor, and Jim described the luxury cars and expensively dressed couples swarming around the hottest nightclubs. Despite the ravages of war, he said, Lebanon's economy was picking up; Beirut was being rebuilt and in all probability Lebanon would regain its former reputation as the "Switzerland of the Near East." In any case, he concluded, safety wouldn't be an issue since I'd be living in Geneva and only traveling periodically to the Middle East. Should the political situation get worse, no one would expect me to expose myself to danger. Now then, he asked, what was my answer?*

With some trepidation, I wrote the decisive e-mail, copying my parents and friends. At 23, I felt like I had hit the big time: I was going to live in Switzerland, travel to exotic countries, and earn a salary that made my eyes pop. I was going to join the ranks of jet-setting young professionals—GenXpats.

> **GenXpat** / 'jen • 'eks • pat / *n.* a member of Generation X, born between 1964 and 1981, who is also an expatriate, or expat; that is, one who decides to live and pursue a career abroad.

GenXpats: Who Are They?

GenXpats are young, internationally and/or culturally mobile professionals. Some begin their adventures by studying abroad and then decide to remain in the foreign country to pursue their careers.

Others are hired by multinationals that are restructuring the way they do business internationally: instead of having local offices in each country, with communication only at the senior management level, many companies are now establishing regional offices that are staffed at all levels with representatives of the member nations. Also, says Jennifer White, Global Client Services Director at Primacy Relocation, there is a greater trend toward developmental assignments, where junior managers are sent abroad for career development—to gain exposure, training, experience, and other desirable management skills. This has become possible as travel and international communication have become increasingly accessible. All in all, rapidly growing numbers of young people are beginning to move and work across nations or cultures.

GenXpats are distinct from the two principal existing types of expats. First, they are different from the "traditional" expat of the past, that is, the senior executive sent abroad with his wife and children on an all-expenses-paid package. They are also unlike the student backpacker, language teacher, or volunteer who is spending an extended time overseas. GenXpats typically set off at a point in their lives when their careers are their top-most consideration and their personal lives are still unsettled. This is what gives rise to some of the unique challenges they face.

◉ *Still single*. GenXpats lack the emotional and logistical support of a spouse, meaning that they must handle all the details of the relocation, learn a new job, and build a social life entirely on their own. Also, their personal lives are still unsettled, so they may have to date abroad, deal with the emotional complexity of a long-distance relationship, or attempt to move with a partner they are not married to, striving to juggle two careers internationally.

 ● *Prone to imbalance and burnout.* When GenXpats head abroad, work is often the only thing to do that is readily available. Recreation and social pursuits all require making an effort in a cuturally foreign setting, and this can be quite intimidating and time consuming, especially without the social setting of a university or the help of a partner. The combination of overwork and few outlets for stress can lead to imbalance or even burnout.

 ● *"Hidden" expats.* GenXpats are often hired as local employees of the country they are in, despite the fact that they are foreigners. As a result, they must live like the locals, and they are more exposed to the local culture than the traditional expat, who can afford to recreate a "home-away-from-home" and socialize in international or diplomatic circles. Also, many of the GenXpats' needs go unnoticed by their employers, such as the fact that they must travel internationally to visit their families and rack up huge phone bills while calling home, or that they need help with the language and understanding the intricacies of local tax laws.

All in all, GenXpats face a unique challenge in terms of their tight finances, the need to juggle work and relocation, more intense cultural exposure, solitude, and a lack of support networks. On top of this, they are confronted with the usual trials of expatriation.

Anyone who goes abroad is confronted with a foreign culture and a different way of doing things, while at the same time losing his or her established lifestyle, hobbies, and social circle.

Expatriates are inevitably thrust out of their comfort zone and often forced to rethink the way they lead their lives. At its best, life abroad can be a catalyst for personal and professional growth. At its worst, it can lead to a sense of lost identity and confusion, as expatriates struggle to make sense of the different possible values and lifestyles they have encountered and try to find meaning in snippets of relationships strewn across the globe, all while flitting from one city or country to another.

It's Your Life

Ideally, as a GenXpat, you should not feel that you must "park" your personal fulfillment as you pursue your professional ambitions abroad. The purpose of this book is to help you find a comfortable balance between the two by providing a framework to adequately prepare for, interpret, and manage your international experience. It examines the following questions:

- *Making the decision:* is living abroad right for you?
- *Contract negotiation:* learning to optimize your contract so that your needs are met abroad.
- *Setting priorities upon arrival:* juggling work, logistics, and adaptation to your new environment.
- *Culture shock:* what is it and how to manage it.
- *Social aspects:* how to build an enriching social life abroad while keeping in touch with those at home.

- *Relationships:* challenges of dating across cultures, long-distance relationships, or moving with your partner.
- *Returning home:* what to do when the home you knew is no longer there...and it won't be.

Too often, as a GenXpat, you can find yourself moving from assignment to assignment without the resources to cope well. You may initially be seduced by the excitement of living abroad, rapid professional advancement, and all-expenses-paid business travel. Eventually, however, the excitement dissipates, all cities seem similarly different, hotel rooms and restaurants blend into uniformity, and your job becomes just that—a job—unless you have the personal context to give it meaning. This book is designed to help you maintain your personal framework and remain satisfied (and sane!) throughout all your relocations.

How "GenXpat" Came to Be

Some of the material for *GenXpat: The Young Professional's Guide to Making a Successful Life Abroad* was inspired by my own experience of living and working in 10 countries in over 10 years. Much comes from my interviews with fellow-GenXpats, both personal friends from around the world and former colleagues. During my time in Geneva, Procter & Gamble simultaneously relocated some 1,000 young managers to its new headquarters, providing me with ample opportunities to interview candidates for every relocation scenario under the sun. Since then, many have moved on to pursue MBAs at prestigious schools like INSEAD, IMD, and Harvard, and others have joined some of the top management consultancies, further adding to their relocation experience. A few are on more individual paths, either pursuing advanced degrees in their fields, founding their own companies abroad, or working as freelancers. The challenges they shared with me were invaluable in shaping the structure of this book, since they indicated the main topics that need to be discussed. The solutions they adopted were crucial for the formulations of dos...and don'ts! Finally, some of their personal stories were so remarkable that I included one at the start of each chapter.

Throwing Down My Anchor

After a decade of living abroad, I decided to return to Canada. My home base is now Vancouver, a 10-hour flight from both Europe and Asia. My work focuses on providing support and resources for the new generation of mobile professionals—I design and implement seminars and training for current and potential GenXpats. On my website, *www.genxpat.com*, you can find a GenXpat forum. I welcome your stories and input!

MAKING THE
DECISION
TO MOVE

1

Zoha, 29, is currently a management consultant in London and has moved internationally six times as an adult. I thought she would be the perfect person to tell me about making the decision to go abroad. She redefined my question at the outset. The decision, she said, is not always yours to make. As a child growing up in war-torn Lebanon in the 1970s, she was often forced to move back and forth to London with her family, depending on the intensity of the conflict. The sorrow involved in a move that you haven't chosen, she explained, is much greater. She remembered saying good-bye to her room, the pain of leaving her friends, school, and extended family behind. However, that is when she began liking travel and relocation despite being forced to do it. She discovered that in a matter of hours of arriving in a new place, she would get excited about the new things sur-rounding her.

Her first deliberate decision to move took place when she chose to pursue her studies at McGill University in Montreal. More than any-thing, this choice was motivated by her desire for change: she wanted to be in a different environment for her studies and to learn new things in a new language. Still, she found it hard to be a 12-hour flight away from her parents and her boyfriend, and she spent her first afternoon crying in front of a huge strawberry milkshake at a McDonald's on Ste-Catherine Street. Fortunately, she wasn't sitting alone. Samer was there, a friend-of-a-friend whom she had called almost instantly upon arriving when a wave of sadness overcame her. The next morning she woke up feeling fine. University life had begun, with the freedom of living alone for the first time, of being in a big city, and enjoying Indian summer—the glorious, crisp, sunny days of September. This pattern was repeated with every subsequent move. The milkshake was replaced by a pâtisserie in Lyon, chocolate in Geneva, and hummus in Lebanon, but Zoha always knew that the next day things would be better—more importantly, bet-ter than before the move. It is this experience of transformation that has kept her moving through the years.

Zoha's rationale for moving evolved over time. The younger she was, the fewer environmental factors she considered. In her early twen-ties, she went on exchange to Lyon because it was the only school that still had space when she applied. She moved to Geneva because she had a job offer there. In essence, she would decide that she wanted to move, then look everywhere and take the best opportunity. Now, when making such a decision, she factors in the type of destination she would like and how it fits with her personal objectives. In her latest relocation, she con-

sidered whether her destination could accommodate her partner's career as well as her own, whether it was safe and secure, and how it would accommodate her lifestyle preferences.

Zoha concluded by discussing the trade-offs involved in moving: inevitably, one ends up choosing the excitement of a new place, as well as the possibilities of an education or a career, over family, friends, familiarity, and stability. Expats always have fantasies of what will happen when they decide to stay in one place. Zoha's was poignant: "When I finally settle down, I'll be able to have cats, dogs, and horses, and personal things-clothes, books, mementos—not restricted to what can fit into a few 70-pound suitcases!"

The Importance of Making an Informed Decision

The first crucial step you need to take before any relocation is making an informed decision about whether to go. As simple as this may sound, the key factors of having a good understanding of your own motivations and setting realistic expectations often determine successful relocations. It is easy to be lured by visions of a new professional challenge or promotion and an exciting life abroad. As tempting as these may be, you also need to consider the flip side of the coin: the long work hours as you master your new job; a foreign, possibly poor or dangerous environment; loneliness; and distance from your family and friends. There will be times when you might be tempted to give up and say, "To hell with it all—I'm going home!" Revisiting your personal objectives for the move can help you survive these moments.

Knowing what you want to achieve with the move also helps you organize your time once you get to your destination. One of the challenges particular to GenXpats is the sheer volume of things to you need to juggle—often just by yourselves: managing the logistics of the move, learning the ropes at work, exploring the host country, making new friends, and keeping in touch with people back home. Setting priorities among all these demands on your time will be easier to do if you have clear objectives. This chapter will help you consider your motivations for going abroad. It will also encourage you to learn more about the external circumstances affecting your move, such as the economic, political, and cultural environment at the destination, and the personal circumstances involved, such as your openness to change or your family situation.

Motivations for Going Abroad

The first item to consider is your motivation for going abroad. Many different possibilities exist and every one is legitimate, though each involves certain inherent risks. We can look at the ones that cropped up the most often in my interviews of GenXpats to get you started in your thinking.

• Professional Advancement
If you are in this group, your main motivation for going abroad is the professional opportunity that lies ahead; you frankly are not that interested in the destination country or city. Rather than

integrate with the local culture, you would prefer to seek out other expats as friends and retain strong ties with home. In your mind, the move is a temporary, though necessary, inconvenience. If this sounds familiar to you, watch out for the possibility of ending up "half-pregnant," that is, not really integrating in the host country and not really being present at home. Straddling locations can have serious consequences. In one extreme case, a senior Procter & Gamble manager spent weekdays in the host country and returned to his home country for weekends because his family did not want to move. The business he was managing suffered because he was not 100 percent present. His family suffered because he was tired from traveling and mentally still occupied by the business he had left behind. He left the company within a year of taking that assignment, completely burnt out.

The bottom line: you must commit mentally to your move for things to work out. If you find yourself thinking of it as a "necessary evil," you might want to find ways to earn your stripes other than relocation.

• *"Checking the Box" of International Experience*

In this day and age, everyone seems to be going abroad, and you feel that you must do the same to avoid getting left behind. You believe that you ought to learn foreign languages, cultures, and business practices because it will strengthen your resumé. In this scenario, be aware of underestimating the commitment involved. Understanding foreign business practices requires observation, reflection, and trial and error; learning a language takes several hours of classes per week plus homework; and even something seemingly as simple as tourism involves planning and effort. And, of course, there are the challenges associated with having to create a new life for yourself abroad, away from your family and friends.

The bottom line: the cultural experience will not fall into your lap. You can expect to get out of your time abroad only what you are willing to put into it. If you are thinking that this is not really of any interest to you, then you may be better off forgoing the foreign experience and doing something that really fascinates you instead.

• *Travel Bug*

There is a huge world out there and you are dying to see it! You are ready to take any foreign assignment just for the sake of experiencing novel sights, sounds, and smells. You plan to learn the language, meet the locals, and even date them if you can; the work you do is secondary. These kinds of objectives may be better suited to a student, part-time work, or volunteer experience abroad. If you plan to go as a serious professional, the demands of your job may be greater than you anticipate and may leave you less time to discover your surroundings than you would like. If you want to maximize your cultural experience, consider whether the nature of your job incorporates some "field" activities. For example, as a marketing professional I had the opportunity to do focus groups, in-home visits, and store checks, all of which let me experience the cultures of the countries I worked in. Some other jobs may only take you on a tour of the offices, airports, hotels, and restaurants of the world without ever experiencing local flavor.

The bottom line: make sure that your travel objectives are compatible with the demands of an international career. Otherwise, you might prefer to save up and take a year off to backpack around the world.

• *Seeking a Better Future*

I have heard people say that anyone who undertakes the challenge of facing the unknown must have experienced some significant dissatisfaction with things as they were at home. This was true in the case of a vivacious, independent Latina GenXpat. She stood out among her fellow nationals, who believed in a more traditional role for women; this led her to seek a more liberal environment in Canada. Her move was an attempt to achieve a closer match between her personal values and those of the surrounding society, and it worked well for her. In other cases, however, the individual idealizes his or her future destination as the key to happiness and the solution to all problems, only to discover that the issues remain even after the relocation, since they were not in the environment but internal, in himself or herself.

The bottom line: you can exchange your society for one whose values more closely match yours, but no relocation can help you run away from your own inner conflicts.

○

You might like to take a minute now to reflect on your own motives for wanting to go abroad. They may relate to one or more

of the reasons listed above. Since your motivations for going
abroad are so critical to your long-term success, don't hesitate to
jot them down here.

1 _____

2 _____

3 _____

External Circumstances to Consider

Another crucial component of the decision to move abroad is to
have a good understanding of the external circumstances you will
be getting into. There are three principal aspects to consider: economic, political, and cultural.

• *Economic Aspects*

Your expatriate experience will be decidedly different depending
if you are going from a first-world country to a third-world one or
the other way around. My first move, from Canada to Poland, was
of the first type. Things I had taken for granted suddenly became
labor-intensive: milk and water had to be boiled before drinking,
getting a telephone line installed was a matter of activating political connections, and the dilapidated buildings required constant
repairs. It was also mentally tiring to be in a place where many are
struggling to make ends meet. By contrast, my move from Poland

to Switzerland represented a vast improvement in my standard of living. To this day, I recall my first weeks in Geneva. It was early December and the Christmas season was in full swing. After the drab streets of Warsaw, the brightly lit and decorated shops appeared magical to me. The challenge there, though, was to avoid getting caught up in the pursuit of the trendiest clothes, cars, and restaurants to the detriment of my bank balance.

How about your move? Will it be an economic "upgrade" or "downgrade" versus your home country? A good way to find out is by checking the CIA World Factbook on the Internet (*www.cia.gov/cia/publications/factbook*). This lists economic indicators about your home country and your destination, such as the Gross Domestic Product (GDP) per capita. Another way is to speak to people who have made the same move as the one you are envisaging and get their first-hand impressions.

• Political Aspects

To most of us living in the Western world, politics does not have a life-and-death significance. This certainly was not what I experienced during my eight months in Israel. Every evening when I turned on the TV, I dreaded seeing the sight of the little explosion icon that indicated the location of yet another terrorist attack. I got used to opening my handbag for inspection before entering a shopping mall, seeing teenagers on leave strolling with M16s slung across their backs, and having my street blocked as a suspect package was being blasted to bits.

There are many different ways in which politics can impact your daily life abroad. In the Near East it was primarily a question of war and physical danger. In some countries, like China, it could be a matter of constant surveillance. Even though you have nothing to hide, it can still be quite debilitating to know that your every intimate moment is being recorded. In a country highly influenced by religious law, like Saudi Arabia, you might find things that you take for granted severely restricted, such as women's rights or freedom of action, dress, or speech. Finally, in a country like Russia, where the mafia is largely unchecked, you might have to ensure your personal safety with bodyguards and heavily secured accommodations.

What is the political situation at your destination? Again, the CIA World Factbook is a good resource, as is the U.S. Department of State website (*www.state.gov/travel/*), and it is imperative to talk with people who have been there to get their first-hand experiences.

• *Cultural Aspects*

Culture is not just about foods or styles of dress, though these can indeed be different from place to place. Culture is also about values—what we view as important and right. Culture shock comes from suddenly discovering that there are other values possible, sometimes diametrically opposed to ours, and that other people hold them to be unquestionably right. This can force us to reconsider our most fundamental assumptions.

Dealing with culture shock is one of the biggest stumbling blocks of moving abroad, and I devote all of Chapter 4 to this. At this stage, however, the objective is only to get a better sense of the types of value differences you will be facing. Probably the most defining aspect of a society is the degree to which individuals are allowed to shape their own fates versus the degree to which families, communities, and religious or political affiliations decide for them. Table 1.1 identifies some basic differences between individualistic societies and group-oriented ones.

Table 1.1 Identifying Cultural Differences

	INDIVIDUALISTIC SOCIETY	GROUP-ORIENTED SOCIETY
VALUES	Freedom to act on individual judgment: "I determine my own fate."	Actions are influenced by the socially acceptable:" My fate is shaped by my family, social, or religious community."
AT WORK	Promotion is based on individual performance.	Promotion is based on family background, group performance, and seniority as well as merit.
AT HOME	People move away from home early to live on their own. Family units are small: only parents and children.	People stay at home until marriage. Family units include grandparents; uncles and cousins are liable to live nearby.

Think about the country you live in and the country you are considering moving to. If you view the two columns in Table 1.1 as extremes, where would your home and host countries fit? If they are similar, then chances are your culture shock will be limited to fairly superficial things such as food and dress. If they are very different, then you are likely to be in for a challenging time. For example, if you believe in promotion based on merit but you are thinking of moving to a country where your colleagues are hired based on their connections, you will need to consider whether you will be comfortable living in a place like this. This does not mean that you need to agree or approve, but you ought to feel confident that can you keep doing business in this way without getting emotionally involved and frustrated. You can find basic cultural descriptions on the Citizenship and Immigration Canada website (*www.settlement.org/cp/english/index.html*). The site is designed to help Canadians understand the cultural background of new immigrants and includes information about the history, family life, work culture, and religion of over 100 countries. Another useful resource is the Geert Hofstede homepage (*www.geert-hofstede.com*), which compares the cultures of over fifty countries in terms of Dr. Hofstede's cultural dimensions.

Having looked at the economic, political, and cultural aspects, you should now be getting a better idea of how different your home and your host country are. In some cases, the differences may rule out your move: you may decide that no job is worth living barricaded in a high-security luxury villa, for example. However, more often than not, the decision will be a question of balancing some inconveniences with the professional advantages of the move.

Personal Circumstances to Consider

Finally, as you consider going abroad, there's a range of personal circumstances to take into account.

• *Leaving Family and Friends*

How big a role do family and friends play in your life? Have you ever gone away from home before for an extended period of time, either to school or to travel around the world? Have you ever lived independently in your own apartment? The reality of moving abroad is that you are likely to find yourself living alone in a place where you don't know anyone. Even if you are very outgoing, it will take time before you find a circle of people you like, and even longer before you move beyond the superficial level of acquaintance into more meaningful friendships. This means that just after arrival, when you are most vulnerable emotionally because of the pressures of work and a new environment, you will be the most isolated. The degree to which you are able to deal with pressure independently, find satisfactory ways of keeping in touch with those you have left behind, and form new friendships will affect how happy you will be with your relocation.

• *Dealing with the Unfamiliar*

Are you a person of habit or do you eagerly seek change? As a child, once I set up the furniture in my bedroom, it would remain in that arrangement until I moved. My best friend did the exact opposite. She would constantly move things around and redecorate her room. As an adult, she craves novelty: she enjoys travel, house-hunting, and moving. For me, every move remains emotionally difficult until I can settle into a regular pattern at my destination. Being aware of your personal style will let you allocate time and resources for effective coping.

• *Romantic Relationships*

If you are single, how will your move impact your ability to meet your match? Remember, you will be in a city where you do not have a network of friends to rely on for introductions. Moreover, you might find yourself in a culture that is very foreign to you, where you might not feel comfortable dating, or where it might not even be possible for you to date (more on this in Chapter 8). If you are currently in a relationship, how do you plan to proceed? Are you willing to break up for the sake of your career? Are you envisaging a long-distance relationship? Will your partner move with you? Are you willing to accept that both of the latter will constitute a major strain on the relationship? (Chapter 9 details some of the challenges of maintaining a long-distance relationship and includes some tips on how to keep one strong.)

• *When You Leave, There Is No Turning Back*

Extended travel exposes you to new ways of doing things, challenges your basic values, and encourages you to grow. The downside is that it may affect your sense of belonging: you may find that you never quite fit in abroad and no longer fit in at home. Are you prepared to deal with this?

Making the Decision

One way to make decisions, especially the ones that are not clear-cut, is to jot everything down on a piece of paper. You might like to start with your motivations for moving, and then continue with the arguments for and against the relocation, keeping in mind some of the points we have covered above. Don't worry about the relative importance of the points; try to focus on getting everything down, even concerns that may seem trivial. Talking things through with a friend can also help you articulate your thoughts. Once you complete the brainstorming phase, then you can sort things as pros and cons and consider listing them in order of importance.

How does your proposed relocation match with your motivation? Do you feel it is a good fit? As you review your list of cons, you may find that there are a lot of question marks rather than pure negatives, such as:

- Will my compensation adequately cover my costs of living abroad?
- Will I be able to adapt to a culture dramatically different from my own?
- Will I be able to build a social life in a country where I do not speak the language?
- My partner does not want to move with me. Should we consider a long-distance relationship?

This is precisely where this book can help: by demystifying corporate contract negotiation policies, helping you identify and understand the different phases of culture shock, giving you practical tips on creating a social life in a foreign country, and sharing relationship adventures. The goal is to give you some real-life perspective on these issues and help you decide whether or not joining the ranks of other GenXpats is the right decision for you.

NEGOTIATING
YOUR CONTRACT

2

*Though Guy, 30, is currently a consultant with Bain & Company in Brussels, our paths crossed when he was a rising star in the Purchasing Department of Procter & Gamble, where he regularly negotiated multimillion-dollar deals with chemical suppliers. At that point, he already had five different employment contracts spanning his four years with the company: a **local new-hire** contract in Belgium, a **local-to-local** package for his transfer to Holland and another for his return to Belgium, a **local-to-expat** relocation to Switzerland, and finally an **expat-to-local** transition while in Geneva. I was convinced that he was the man to tell me all about the strategies for negotiating employment contracts. (These terms are described later in this chapter.)*

Guy seemed genuinely astonished when I brought this up. He confessed that he had never felt that much negotiation was possible when it came to the terms of his employment. The offers had always been presented in the spirit of "take it or leave it." Besides, he had found it hard to predict ahead of time what a package meant in net terms, and thus what he should negotiate. For example, as a new graduate he was offered an elaborate mix of salary, pension plan, stock purchase program, and medical benefits. None of this meant much to him at the time —he was simply glad to have an income after the lean years as a university student. Later, during his local transfer to Holland, he found it challenging to compare his Belgian salary with the one he was offered in Rotterdam given the difference in salary progression, tax rates, and cost of living. It was only when he was going to return to Belgium that he knew to focus on maximizing his relocation bonus, as any salary improvements would be marginal in comparison.

When P&G decided to create a new European, Middle East, and African headquarters in Geneva, Guy was one of over a thousand employees from the United Kingdom, Belgium, and Germany to be offered a lucrative two-year expat package in exchange for moving on short notice. He noted that work practically stopped in the months preceding the relocation, as people worried about optimizing their career prospects, income, and family considerations. Rumors abounded. Some people claimed to have negotiated special deals for themselves despite the supposedly standard packages available. Guy wondered whether this was in fact the case or whether it was smart maneuvering on the part of the HR folks, who offered small concessions now at the price of future salary increases. He decided to stay clear of the speculation and focused on his work instead. While others were distracted by the nego-

tiations and the relocation, he delivered his projects with excellence. Eventually, this turned out to be the best strategy: it earned him a promotion, a better rating, and ultimately a more aggressive salary curve.

Another lesson came during the **expat-to-local** *transition, also known as "localization." Visions for the shift from generous expat packages, which included housing, a car, and cost-of-living allowances, to the simple salary of a Swiss local had never been well defined. The company mentioned lump-sum transition bonuses and other measures, but nothing specific. The bottom line amounted to "trust us." When the numbers turned out to be less than imagined, it was hard to point fingers; after all, no commitment had been made. However, for Guy it highlighted the importance of the written document as the best foundation for trust.*

Some months later, Guy left P&G to try his hand at management consulting. The interview and contract negotiation process at top consulting firms is the stuff of legends, so I was curious to hear how things had gone. Guy reported that he began by looking at things strategically, opting to start at a lower level in the firm and at a more modest salary, with the prospect of earning a better performance rating, a higher bonus, and faster salary progression. He expected this approach to yield a better long-term return than starting at the next rung up in the company hierarchy. He was initially offered a salary and a performance-based annual bonus, which, by now, he knew better than to try to negotiate. Instead, he focused on getting an additional one-time starting bonus, sufficient to cover his relocation expenses. It made sense on many levels: these were items that his employer could easily write off as expenses, and they translated into cash-in-hand for him. Finally, he insisted on getting—ahead of time—the fine print of his contract and a plan for the transition from the Swiss system of holidays, pensions, and insurances to the Belgian one. This let him make sure that his employer would commit to cover any gaps, and that this commitment could be captured in his contract.

When I remarked that he did, after all, have insights to share, Guy insisted that he hadn't yet felt fully on top of things despite having had many turns at contract negotiation. Perhaps, we reflected, it's unreasonable to expect that as young managers we can wholly dictate our own terms. With time, though, we can certainly learn to ask the right questions and tailor our offers in that way.

Win-Win

Whether you are already an employee and are negotiating your package to go abroad, or if you are discussing the terms of your contract with a new employer in a foreign country, the process can certainly be stressful. You may be tempted to make this a match of wits: "How much can I get? Can I get more than so-and-so?" Be aware that this attitude can take your attention off the work at hand, and this can put you behind schedule. Also, though you may "win" the negotiation process by getting a promotion or lucrative contract, it can mean an increased workload and higher expectations from your employer. The combination of scrambling to catch up and feeling the pressure to deliver results can turn the inherently hectic process of relocation into a nightmare.

You can set yourself up more favorably by seeking *win-win* solutions that benefit both you and your employer. To do so, however, you must have a good understanding of your employer's perspective and of your own needs for living abroad. This chapter will give you some insight into the corporate mindset, starting with a discussion of the principles that guide compensation design, continuing with different expat contract types, and concluding with typical areas for negotiation by contract type. It will also help you assess your needs so that you can build your strategy around the particularities of your own situation, rather than trying to match what others have negotiated or attempting to wrangle the most money out of your employer.

How Employers Think about Compensation

As a company prepares an offer, one factor it considers is how the offer relates to the market. Most multinationals buy salary benchmarking data pertaining to their "peer group" of companies and decide how they would like to position themselves with regard to this: the top, middle, or bottom of the range. While some will want to pay top dollar to get the best talent, others aim for average compensation and count on other factors, such as their reputation and the training they can offer, to attract candidates. Small companies also conduct comparisons, but much more informally, getting a sense for the market price of talent through a combination of trial and error and networking.

Once a firm has decided on a compensation strategy with regard to external factors, it must consider how its compensation packages will relate to each other internally. Ideally, compensation needs to reflect both the performance and seniority of employees, and its principles must be equitable, standardized, and transparent. This is fairly easy with a small office in one location. It gets more challenging when dealing with hundreds of offices across the globe and with employees in countries with different standards of living.

Many multinationals resolve this dilemma by creating salary ranges based on seniority and performance for each country they operate in. For example, depending on performance, a Swiss brand manager with four years of experience might make between USD 75,000 and 92,000, while her Canadian equivalent might earn USD 50,000 to 70,000. The monetary difference is a function of external factors, such as market conditions and the cost of living in the two countries. However, internal "fairness" is maintained in that all people at this level of seniority in a particular country will fall within the specified range.

Compensation across Borders

What happens during relocation, then? There are two principal compensation scenarios: moving as an expat and moving as a local. Let's look at each one in more detail.

If the Swiss brand manager we considered earlier were to move from Switzerland to Canada as an *expat,* it would mean that her home base would remain in Switzerland: she would be considered a Swiss employee sent abroad on assignment. She would retain her

Swiss pay and benefits, though the salary itself would be adjusted for differences in the cost-of-living and hardship. Since Canada is generally cheaper to live in than Switzerland, chances are her Swiss pay would be adjusted downwards (multiplied by a factor of 0.85, for example). Also, since Canada is not politically more volatile or dangerous than Switzerland, there would likely be no hardship allowance (the hardship factor would be 1.0). Whenever her salary would be reviewed, it would be compared to the Swiss salary range appropriate to her performance and seniority. The idea is that when she returns to Switzerland and all the cost-of-living and hardship factors are removed, she should still be within the same salary range as her peers—thus ensuring that fairness is maintained.

If, on the other hand, the Swiss brand manager were to make the move as a *local*, it would mean that she would be transferring her corporate home base from Switzerland to Canada: she would henceforth be considered a Canadian employee. For this reason, she would have to consider an offer in the USD 50,000 to 70,000 salary range that is appropriate to her peer group in Canada, again to maintain fairness.

Negotiability of Different Compensation Components

Now you can see why most large, formally structured companies are fairly constrained in terms of the range of salary figures they can offer a candidate. Straying outside the prescribed range for a given level of performance and seniority could jeopardize their desired position within the general employment market and could affect their internal system of fairness as well. This standardized approach also applies to benefits, such as pension plans, health insurance, and stock purchase programs, as well as expat packages. Jennifer White, Global Client Services Director of Primacy Relocation, explains that she encourages her clients to have a global policy that establishes uniform principles for each type of expat assignment. It is important, she says, that a company provide equal benefits to its employees and not negotiate basic benefits on a case-by-case basis.

At the same time, employers need a bit of leeway when they wish to woo an attractive candidate. In such cases, the preference is usually toward one-time items that do not jeopardize the ongoing system of fairness and that can be written off as expenses, such as a lump sum to cover start-up costs in a new location, services like relocation and tax counseling, or even perks such as a budget for travel home. White confirms that some degree of flexibility also exists with respect to standard expat policies. She encourages her clients to acknowledge the changing profile of their expat populations, especially the growing number of dual-career couples associated with the increase in GenXpats. Career assistance for the accompanying partner is a critical benefit, and it is a valid negotiating point if it is not offered in the global policy.

Another thing to keep in mind during negotiation is the tax environment. In Switzerland, for example, the income tax is fairly low, so the bulk of employee compensation is paid in cash, as salary, or a year-end bonus. By contrast, in countries like Poland and Israel, where taxes are very high, there is an incentive for companies to offer lower salaries together with in-kind compensation, such as a car or cell phone for both work-related and private use. The employer can write these off as expenses, while as an employee you benefit by getting taxed only on your low salary while getting use of the car or the phone tax-free. Becoming familiar with the kind of tax environment you are heading to will help you understand the rationale for the mix of cash and in-kind benefits you are offered, and this will enhance your negotiation efforts. For example, while it may make sense to negotiate a higher bonus in Switzerland, aiming for cash in Poland will only put more tax dollars into the government's pocket (and less into yours).

Demystifying Corporate Relocation Packages

Relocation packages are not the mysterious treasure chests they are made out to be. By and large, they have been designed with the interests of both the employer and the employee in mind. From the employer's perspective, the principal distinction is whether the company or the employee is initiating the move. If the company needs an individual's expertise abroad, then it is often willing to pay any amount to get her to move promptly and to ensure that her personal needs are met at the destination, leaving the employee free to focus on work. This type of compensation is usually called an *expat package*. On the other hand, if the employee requests to transfer to a foreign office or is hired outside her home country, then the employer considers that there is no reason to compensate the employee for the trouble of moving, other than perhaps to cover the cost of transit. This scenario is usually called a *local package*, since the employee is hired abroad on the same terms as a local employee.

Expat packages can be further broken down into two types: long term and short term. This distinction is important for tax and residency reasons. Typically, you are considered a resident and tax payer of the country that you spend six or more months per year in. This means that you can remain a resident of your home country and travel on business to another country for up to half a year without any paperwork other than a tourist visa. As soon as you plan to spend more than six months per year at your destination, the local authorities will start to consider you a resident of their country, require that you get a work/residency permit, and expect you to begin paying taxes there.

Long-Term Expat Packages

Let us begin by considering what can give rise to the need for expat employees. In the classic scenario, high-flying senior managers are sent to foreign outposts to share expertise, drive the business, and keep operations in line with corporate policy. Exposing these managers to different markets is also meant to groom them for executive positions that oversee regional or global operations. Companies design the relocation packages of these individuals to make the move as unnoticeable as possible and to ensure that they can focus their energy on delivering results. The guiding principle behind such long-term expat packages is "re-creating a home away from home," meaning that an expat usually receives the following:

- The same net salary as at home, adjusted for the cost of living and hardship of the posting
- A refund of relocation costs, such as travel, shipment of personal effects, and legal paperwork
- Compensation for selling her home and car on short notice and unfavorable terms
- Housing and car allowances at the destination, to compensate for the need to purchase on short notice and unfavorable terms
- Paid schooling for children in their mother tongue or in English, usually in private international schools
- An annual trip home
- Assistance in procuring the foreign work permit and residency papers, as well as tax and financial advice

This is obviously a very attractive deal, but it is also an expensive one for the employer. Companies primarily use this package when they ask an employee to go on foreign assignment in a dangerous or underdeveloped location, or when the employee does not want to move but her skills are needed abroad. An expat contract typically lasts at least 12 months, and more likely upwards of 24 months, because of the hassle involved in relocating a family and changing legal residence to another country.

Short-Term Expat Packages

Sometimes the employer needs to transfer skills from one location to another on a short-term or project basis. As Jennifer White explains, this type of expat contract is on the rise because it fills a business or developmental need without requiring the relocation of a family or of personal effects and, as such, it represents a significant reduction in costs versus the traditional long-term expat package. And since the employer is initiating the move, it designs an attractive compensation package. The principle here is that the employee keeps her legal residence, as well as her house, car, and family in the home country but spends weeks at a time at destination. A typical short-term expat package lasts less than a year in total and includes the following:

- Lodging in a residential hotel (usually a suite with a kitchenette)
- Per diem allowance to cover expenses (usually meals, laundry, and gas for a rental car)
- Rental car
- Frequent travel home (depending on the employer, distance, and family situation, up to twice a month)

Both of these options—long- and short-term expat packages—used to be reserved for senior management. However, the increased globalization of business combined with cheap travel and communications are now bringing international work within the responsibilities of middle managers as well. These are individuals with a few years' work experience with their current employer and probably at least one promotion that testifies to their proven track record. The principal challenge companies face as mid-level expats proliferate is the question of costs. Expat packages with full trimmings cost up to three times the employee's regular salary. That is why you will find increasing attempts on the part of employers to create modified expat packages that are a hybrid between the traditional all-expenses-paid scenario and a local transfer, which we will look at next.

Foreigners on Local Packages

New hires and junior managers are unlikely to be sent abroad on expensive expat packages as they rarely have experience that cannot be supplied by a cheaper local employee. Thus, if you are hired outside your home country or are sent abroad a few months into your job, your employer will most likely offer you the same terms as would be proposed to a local. Similarly, if you ask to relocate abroad to gain experience or for personal reasons, chances are the employer will also provide a *local contract*, since the foreign posting is to your benefit.

Let us examine the circumstances that can lead to a foreigner being hired with a local package. Not surprisingly, the most frequent scenario involves foreign students looking for employment in the country where they completed their university degrees. Employers usually consider foreign graduates in the same light as local ones. In another case, a company may be staffing a regional operation with citizens of the various countries it subsumes, and handling senior employees as expats while offering local packages to junior managers and new hires. White explains that hiring foreigners on local packages in this way is most likely to occur among countries on one continent, for example between Canada and the U.S., intra-Europe, or intra-Asia, rather than between continents. Usually, employers design a local package to cover the following:

- Travel expenses to the destination
- Expenses related to legalities, such as work permits
- Temporary accommodation until you find a place to stay
- Cost of shipping your personal effects

Apart from local and expat packages, there are the infrequent occasions when an employer wishes to downgrade a compensation package. Usually this occurs when an individual has exhausted the prescribed term for an expat contract and is given the option to become a *local*, that is, to "localize," or to return to his home country. Localization usually involves some sort of a cash bonus to soften the transition from the elaborate benefits of an expat to the more modest local living package.

The Negotiation Process: Strategy

The negotiation process involves essentially two phases for both new hires and employees being transferred. In the first, strategic phase, you need to consider and weigh your career prospects, as well as your desired location and compensation package. Once you have these major building blocks in place, you can proceed to negotiate the fine print and the specifics of your situation.

As a new hire, the strategic phase of negotiation looks much like it did for Guy when he discussed the terms of his employment with Bain & Company. He had the option of accepting a lower position in the hierarchy, with more modest compensation initially but with greater potential to do well and rise quickly, or to push for a fancier title and more money, while setting the bar of expectations higher. There is no right or wrong way to do this; in fact, the correct way may be culturally influenced. In the U.S., promotion is performance based, and your employer may feel more comfortable hiring you at a lower level, allowing you to prove yourself briefly, and then promoting you quickly. In countries more concerned with proper respect for seniority or hierarchy, it would be an unthinkable degradation to get hired below your level, and it would also be impossible for you to be promoted through the ranks faster than others.

If you are considering relocation with your current employer, this usually means that you are at a career crossroads and are looking for a new assignment. There are typically three things you will be trying to achieve: more money, a promotion, or a learning experience that will ultimately lead to more of both. Depending on how well you are doing, your employer will be more or less eager to grant you a mix of these.

In one situation, a colleague of mine was hired abroad and performed very well, but she was still quite junior when the company needed her expertise back home. She was not particularly eager to move back—her home country was in political turmoil—so the company needed to provide an incentive for her to do so. The company considered early promotion as one option and a lucrative expat package as another, but these were particularly hard to justify given her lack of seniority and the fact that she was a native of the country in question. Finally, my colleague suggested that she would move as a local and take a pay cut in exchange for an early promotion and more responsibility. She also stipulated that, if she continued to do well, she would only stay for two years in her home country and later be sent to all other company locations as an expat. This is exactly what happened. Her strategy was very sound: by initially accommodating the company financially and by delivering superb results, she built up a great deal of good will. When her two years were up, the company felt obligated to keep its end of the deal. My colleague benefited immensely by her long-term, balanced approach.

The Negotiation Process: The Fine Print

Once you have a general agreement in place, you may be tempted to immediately start negotiating the fine print of your contract. Before you rush into that, however, it makes a lot of sense to request a *Look-See Trip* to your destination. This trip helps you build a better picture of the economic, political, and cultural environment you will be moving to, get a feel for the kind of neighborhood you would like to live in and the price of housing there, decide whether you will need a car, and so on. All this information will help you identify your needs and present a stronger case as you discuss the details of your contract. Normally your employer should agree to this trip, as it is a small, one-time expense compared to the potential loss incurred by an unsuccessful relocation. Even if your employer does not sponsor you, it is absolutely worth your while to go at your own expense. For ideas on how to make the most of your Look-See Trip, refer to Appendix A.

Once you return, you will be ready to sit down and review your employer's proposal. If your agreement was, for example, that you will be moving abroad as an expat, you can expect the company to give you a standard document detailing the cost-of-living and hardship factors applicable to your destination, as well as your housing, car, and school allowances. You can think of this second phase of negotiation as personalizing an "off-the-shelf" proposal. For instance, if you don't plan to have a car but would like to overspend your housing budget by 10 percent, you may be able to make such an adjustment. In the next few sections we will look at how you can adapt a standard contract to your needs.

Adapting a New-Hire Contract

Let's imagine that you are Polish, have just graduated from a university in France, and have gotten an offer from a French employer. As Poland is now a member of the European Union, your employer sees no reason to treat you differently than a French candidate, and offers you a local salary plus relocation costs.

The first challenge you face is assessing the net value of the offer. At first glance, you realize that a starting French salary of €80,000 (USD 100,000) is much more than what you could earn in Poland, but it is important to figure out what will be left in your pocket after taxes and unemployment, pension, and health contributions, and after taking into account the higher cost of living in France. While you can ask your employer about the deductions, estimating the cost of living (COL) abroad is your biggest issue. Existing Web-based resources are fairly limited. The free COL calculators focus primarily on the United States and Canada, and simply translate your current salary into its supposed "equivalent" at destination, while entirely ignoring the issue of your lifestyle and spending patterns. There are some international COL calculators, but these usually provide data by country, and that too can be unreliable: the cost of living in Paris has nothing to do with the cost of living in the rest of France.

To help you estimate these expenses, I created a homegrown COL calculator (see Appendix B). This COL calculator draws on data that you can easily collect: your monthly budget breakdown at home, as well as your salary, tax rate, and rent at destination, together with the cost of a taxi ride and a few food staples, all of which you can gather during your Look-See Trip. I've checked it against all the different places I've lived in and it has proven reliable.

Once you establish how the salary component of your new-hire contract abroad relates to your lifestyle and financial objectives, you can decide whether you want to negotiate. As we

saw earlier, salary figures are quite constrained by fairness considerations, so you can only expect to negotiate by a few percent. You
are more likely to benefit by attempting to broaden the scope of
what your employer considers your one-time relocation costs,
beyond the usual travel, temporary accommodation, and shipping of personal effects. In general, your argument should focus
on one-time expenses you are incurring due to the move that
would not otherwise occur. These include:

○ *Financial and tax advice.* One of the hairiest things involved
in a local move is that your financial transition is not the responsibility of the company—it is yours. You have to find out about tax
treaties between your home and host countries. This is usually
pretty convoluted, and a run-of-the-mill accountant will not be
able to help you. You might have to turn to a firm that specializes
in relocation financial management, and this comes at a price.

○ *Language lessons.* You speak English at work, but it would
be nice to be able to read the labels on your groceries, give the cab-
driver directions, or order your dinner in the local language. You
can request your employer to cover several months' worth of language lessons to get you up to speed.

○ *Purchase of new furnishings.* If this is your first "real" job
after your student years, you will likely to want to upgrade
your futon to something a little more respectable.

○ *Purchase of a new wardrobe.* You may be trading your student jeans for business suits, or moving from a tropical country to
ice-cold Canada. Either way, you will need to do a one-time shopping spree.

A number of other things will be impacted by the move: your phone bill is likely to explode because of the international phone calls you will make, you will want to travel home for holidays, and you will not be as savvy a shopper as your local colleagues. Sadly, requests for help with these kinds of expenses are not likely to convince your employer: they are recurring and hard to quantify. Still, it is good to be aware of them for your own budgeting purposes.

Finally, an important thing to ask about is your benefits. You will want to compare the number of vacation days you would normally have in your home and host countries, and the kinds of medical, dental, travel, accident, disability, maternity, and unemployment insurances that are usually covered either by your government or your employer. When you move as a local, you typically need to accept the standards of your destination country. However, if these standards vary greatly from what you would get at home, you can try to get some help from your employer in this respect.

Adapting a Local-to-Local Contract

We have just looked at what happens when you are hired abroad as a local. If you are already employed, you are most likely to be sent abroad as a local by your employer if you are fairly junior, if you have some connection to your destination (e.g., a dual citizenship), or if you request the move. In the classic local-to-local transfer scenario, your employer covers your relocation costs and determines your salary within the appropriate seniority and performance range at destination. If you find the amount increasing—great! If, on the other hand, you see it decreasing, there is not much you can do in terms of the salary itself because of the fairness issues discussed earlier. However, if your salary is going down, it usually means you are going from a more developed country to a less developed one, and possibly to a place where your employer has a hard time finding qualified local candidates.

If you agree to go as a local, you are accommodating your employer. Hopefully, you have already used this leverage to secure some career advantages, such as increased responsibility or a promotion. You can further try to secure some one-time financial advantages, beyond the ones mentioned in the previous section. Here are two options:

1. *A "soft landing," or cash bonus, designed to ease your transition.* I've seen this calculated as the difference between the annual salary in country of origin and that at destination, paid out as a lump sum. The justification was that it would allow transferees to make a down payment for a house in their home country or cover other set-up costs, making the salary cut less painful.

2. *Benefits related to family status.* If you are leaving your partner behind, you can argue for a "split-family" package that allows regular visits for both of you. Even though this can appear to be a recurring expense, it would usually be handled as an annual travel budget awarded on a one-time basis each year. If your partner is moving with you, you can ask that your employer help with language lessons, work permit formalities, and job-hunting services.

Again, considering these arrangements up front is critical in your decision making.

Adapting a Short- or Long-Term Expat Contract

It is an open secret that you only start earning "big bucks" as a salaried employee of a multinational when you get sent on an expat contract. This is because your net salary is maintained (modified for COL and hardship at destination), while your relocation costs, financial advice, lodging, car, schooling, and trips home are paid by your employer, so you basically get to squirrel away your whole income! This is one of the situations where it can be risky to ask for more money or bonuses because it can create ill will. There is nothing wrong, however, with trying to tailor the amount offered to best suit your needs. You are best off aiming for one if not both of the following:

1. *Flexibility of your allowances.* Let's say that a standard expat contract with your employer provides an allowance for housing, car, and schooling abroad. Since you are single and plan to live downtown, you would prefer to get a more generous housing budget in exchange for giving up the car and schooling benefits. It is quite likely that you can negotiate this. Be careful, however, if you plan to underspend your allowances in the hope of pocketing the difference—this is rarely permitted.

2. *Benefits related to family status.* Similar to the case of being sent abroad as a local, if your expat contract takes you away from your family, you can request more frequent trips home. If your family moves with you, you should aim to get as much support for their relocation as you can (see the previous section).

You may be wondering if the COL and hardship factors applied to your base salary are negotiable. Unfortunately, it is highly unlikely that they would be. Large corporations usually purchase this kind of data from relocation consultancies and use it for all relocations company-wide. Sometimes the numbers do not seem to reflect reality, but your employer is not in a position to do anything about this. If she were to make an exception for you, then it would jeopardize the fairness of the system for others.

By contrast, small companies do not usually have set guidelines regarding benefits that are due to an expat or about the appropriate COL factors. If you are facing a situation where things are undefined, it may be a good idea to suggest to your employer that she hire relocation consultants to do the calculations and recommend benefits. If you allow your employer to do the work, and if she hasn't had experience living abroad, she may not realize the costs involved. If you do the work, your employer may not buy into your calculations of COL differences.

○

In summary, you should begin your negotiation by assessing your situation: Are you in the position of having a strong track record and proven performance, such that you can set certain terms with your employer, or are you the one in the weaker position, either because you are a new hire, quite junior, or requesting to move for personal reasons? In the first case, you have the opportunity to try and secure some benefits, such as a promotion, an expat contract, or a particularly interesting challenge or location, though it is probably best to focus just on one of these rather than all of them together. In the latter case, it is probably helpful to recognize that in all likelihood you will be transferred as a local.

Once you have secured the big picture, the next step is to go check out your destination, to help prepare you for negotiating the fine print of your contract. At that stage, you are most likely to succeed in your negotiation if you ask for modifications that are a result of the demonstrable particulars of your situation. Best of luck in your efforts!

JUGGLING WORK
AND LOGISTICS
ON ARRIVAL

The glass doors slid open with a slight rattle and my steps echoed on the stone floor within. The lobby was an expanse of green marble and polished steel, broken only by a silver relief of the P&G logo above the receptionist's desk. I introduced myself and sank down on the black leather seats, a little awed.

Shortly thereafter, the HR manager came to greet me and led me to her office. Handing me a thick binder, she launched into an explanation of the paperwork that needed to get done: I had to review and sign my employment contract, and fill out forms for my pension plan, stock plan, health insurance, and corporate credit card applications. These were to be done by the end of the week. I was also to familiarize myself with the dress code, vacation policy, and rules on making personal phone calls from the office. She then drew out four densely printed sheets that looked like a list. She explained that this was a summary of the most frequent P&G acronyms, created for the sake of poor souls like myself, who have a hard time deciphering what their colleagues are saying. Feeling a little dazed, I followed her on a tour of the building, trying to remember the location of key facilities. Finally, we ended up in front of my boss' office.

He welcomed me and motioned me to sit down. With great enthusiasm, he picked up a stack of documents and explained what they were as he placed them on the desk in front of me: the annual business review, strategic planning documents, sales results, and a Category Assessment Study (CAS). The pile was over a foot high. My assignment in the next month, he told me, was to use these to learn the dynamics of the market, identify key opportunities, and create an action plan. The first two documents seemed to be composed primarily of acronyms and numbers, while the CAS was a 200-page printout of Always™ market share split by product type (Thick and Ultra), religion (Muslim, Christian, and Druze), as well as geographic area (Beirut, the Bekaa Valley, and North, Central, and South Lebanon). I felt a rising wave of panic as I realized that I had no idea what any of this meant.

Misinterpreting my wide-eyed look for one of eagerness, he smiled and reminded me that I should not focus single-mindedly on my work. It was equally important for me to make sure I got all the logistics out of the way in a timely fashion. He could forgive me for taking extended house-hunting lunch breaks for now, he said, but not a few months down the road. Since midday was fast approaching, he sug-gested that I meet the rest of the team and join them for lunch.

As I had joined the Near East Group, there followed a slew of for-eign and unretainable names: Zeina, Ilan, Dor, Arnon, Hounaida, Ori... We headed down to the cafeteria amid a chatter of Hebrew and Arabic. I sensed it was a matter of pride that they were all working together despite regional tensions. At the same time, I realized that I had a lot to learn about the area before I could work effectively.

The afternoon greeted me with a throbbing headache and an appointment with the technical department. I was provided with a lap-top and introduced to the key proprietary P&G software. My mind was so saturated with new information at this point that I could only stare and nod blankly. I finally got home to an empty fridge after a 12-hour workday. I went straight to bed and slept right through until morning. This scenario repeated almost daily for well over a month.

Main Demands on Your Time upon Arrival

If you need an overview of relocation logistics, I refer you to *The Expert Expatriate* by Melissa Brayer Hess and Patricia Linderman (Nicholas Brealey Publishing/Intercultural Press, 2002). Written with the accompanying spouse in mind, it does an excellent job of covering pre-departure preparation including visas, health issues, packing strategies, and how to set up your financial affairs so that you can manage them at a distance. It does not, however, discuss the one challenge particular to GenXpats: how to manage the combined demands of working and moving when there is no spouse or partner to help you.

Let's start by taking a look at the most urgent demands on your time when you arrive, in order of chronology and importance:

1. *Figuring out your new environment.* The geography (how to get to and from the office), money (how to obtain cash), and food/laundry (you may be in a residential hotel where you must cook and launder for yourself) all fall into this category.

2. *Learning the ropes at work.* You'll need to begin by understanding your new responsibilities and objectives, meeting new colleagues, and getting set up with computer systems and office procedures.

3. *Taking care of logistics.* The first phase, lasting a month or so, includes obtaining your work permit, finding a place to live, getting set up with a bank account and credit card, transferring to local health insurance, getting your driver's license, and signing up for company benefits. The second phase usually occurs in about Month 3, when you move into your apartment and need to get set up with utilities, receive your furniture shipment, and shop for whatever is missing.

Apart from all of this, you will likely want to keep in touch with the family and friends you have left behind, de-stress through some sort of exercise, start discovering the new city and country you are in, make new acquaintances, and start learning the local language. Where do you begin?

Setting Priorities in the First Month

Rather than simply trying to cram as much as possible into your day, it makes sense to set priorities based on what is absolutely essential to the success of your stay and what can wait for some time. Here are some thoughts on how you may like to approach things, and why.

With regard to the first point—figuring out your environment—it can be helpful to arrive at your destination early in the weekend, or even on the last day of the week before you actually start work, during business hours. That way you have the time to unpack and go grocery shopping at your leisure, and to figure out how to get to work on Monday morning. Remember to bring quite a bit of cash in the local currency with you—never assume that your ATM card or credit card will work abroad. Another good idea is to have the home contact information of a future colleague or your HR manager, so you can contact someone for help if you really get stuck.

The next most pressing issues are learning the ropes at work and dealing with logistics. Your job is, clearly, what has brought you abroad, and doing it well is crucial to the success of your stay. What may be less obvious is the importance of attending to logistical issues promptly. The rationale is simple: your work permit or visa is what allows you to remain legally in a country, and non-completion of the required paperwork and payments could cause the authorities to send you home and mean a fine for your employer. Moreover, you usually need your permit papers for any subsequent steps, such as opening a bank account, which in turn is essential for signing a lease. House hunting is worth moving quickly on, too. As a senior manager pointed out to me, the first month is a time when you are being paid to learn and ask questions rather than deliver results, and as such it is a window of opportunity to get yourself set up on the personal end of things. If you postpone house hunting until three or four months into the game—it happens—then you are distracted with moving at a time when people are starting to look at your performance and results.

So what should be your focus at work during the first month? It is useful to get a clear mandate from your boss, in writing, outlining your top work priorities and when you need to deliver them. This will help you understand what you should and, equally importantly, should not be working on, thus freeing up time for logistics. A good boss will give you an "early win" opportunity, that is, a project that you can reasonably accomplish and do well at during your first month on the job, one that lets you get an overview of the business, meet key people, and gain credibility. If your boss does not do this, take a look at your top three priorities and see if one can fit the bill. As much as possible, focus your energies on that one project, on asking all possible questions about the business, computer systems, and infrastructure, and on identifying the colleagues who are your best resources to get your work done. Accomplishing this in a quality way will get you more credibility than trying to do everything at once, and it will ideally allow you time to manage your logistics in parallel.

Striving for Balance

The amount of time you spend at work in the initial days sets the tone and the expectations for the future. From the very first day, one of my most successful colleagues never stayed later than 6:00 P.M., though he may have done quite a bit of work at home. Because he delivered excellent results, his "early" departure was never questioned, and in fact people grew to expect it and respect it: everyone knew that it was useless to schedule a meeting where his presence was required after a certain hour. If at all possible, try to avoid the temptation of putting in long hours at the office to prove yourself. A timely departure not only encourages you to balance your lifestyle from the very beginning, but it also prevents you from setting a precedent that you will be expected to sustain.

The huge amount of novelty in the first month can be exhausting. In the first days your brain is overloaded with stimuli and nothing is automatic—not even finding and using the copy machine or buying a cup of coffee. Each of these formerly innocuous activities seems to require as much attention and effort as your decision to move abroad! Do not despair—you will eventually settle into a daily routine that will free up your mind to deal with more complex issues. In the meantime, however, you may find yourself requiring more rest than usual. Listen to your body: make sure you get enough sleep. Many GenXpats report that they need up to 12 hours of sleep a night during the first couple of weeks abroad. Also, though it may feel like the last thing you need given your exhaustion, doing light exercise is a natural way to reduce your stress level and improve your subsequent focus. It can be something as simple as a brisk walk to work. In cities not conducive to outdoor activity, getting a gym membership early on may be a wise move (this is also a great way to meet people).

Things That Can Be Done Later

Given that you have work, logistics, extra rest, and moderate exercise overfilling your first weeks, you will need to postpone some things. Here are some of the things that may be possible to put off.

● *Keeping in touch with people back home.* Hard as it may seem, the first few months are not the time to be spending hours communicating with those you have left behind, and certainly not the moment to receive a visit from Mom and Dad. Take the time to say proper good-byes before you leave, and let people know that you will be out of touch for the first little while; telling them this manages their expectations. Once you get to your destination, you can write a mass e-mail to let everyone know you are all right and then send mass periodic updates. In Chapter 6, we will look in more detail at how you can prioritize whom you keep in touch with, so that you do maintain essential relationships without drowning trying to keep in touch with everyone.

● *Creating a social life at destination.* Using your lunch breaks to get to know your colleagues and to build a support network is a good idea, but carefully balance this with the other calls on your lunchtime, such as paperwork and house-hunting. As for purely social activities your colleagues might invite you to, such as drinks after work, indulge in them only to the extent that they don't interfere with your priorities. You don't necessarily have to appear anti-social; you can explain that you have a lot going on and that you will be more than happy to participate once you have things sorted out. One way of signaling your return on the social scene after the initial set-up phase is by throwing a house-warming party. You can initiate building a social life outside of work, by joining clubs and other community activities, once the time is right.

○ *Tourism.* You might find your first weekends occupied with housekeeping activities and catching up on sleep, and later with unpacking your shipment and setting up your apartment, so it is probably unrealistic to expect that you will have "done" all the major tourist spots in the first month at your destination. That being said, it is worth being disciplined about all the logistical activities to ensure that you do have the time to discover the country, especially to the extent that it contributes to your work. When I was working in Israel, touring the different regions significantly contributed to my understanding the way of life of minority groups such as Arab Israelis and Orthodox Jews, and this was crucial to designing effective marketing campaigns.

○ *Competitive sports and time-intensive hobbies.* You may have been doing triathlons in your free time back home and logging multiple training hours a day. It could be that, in deciding to pursue an international career, you may have to make a choice to focus initially on your work and your new environment rather than on your hobbies. Be aware that it usually takes about six

months to get your work under control and your basic routine settled to the point where you can focus on other things.

   ● *Language lessons.* Unless the language is a crucial factor for
your success at work, chances are that you will not have
enough time to devote to studying it in the initial months. Most
of my colleagues in Geneva who got company-sponsored French
lessons ended up canceling them due to lack of time and irregu-
lar schedules. Your chances for sustained attendance will be far
greater once you are settled into your new home and have established a routine. On the other hand, if you find that you are
having a hard time functioning without knowing the language—
for example, you can't read your bills or go shopping because
everything is in Greek—then you have a bigger problem that cannot be addressed by language lessons after work. Try asking a
colleague to help, or even ask your employer about getting assistance from one of the support staff. Don't avoid the problem,
though. One of my colleagues simply ignored the letters he
received from the Swiss authorities because he did not understand French, and he almost lost his work permit and accrued all
sorts of penalty fees.

These were the priority calls I made; yours may well be different
depending on the nature of your work and interests. For example, a
diplomat may have language training and building social networks
as part of the job description, with fewer projects than a businessperson. You might like to take a moment to write down what
you consider to be the key things you need to focus on during the

first six months on the job. Whenever you feel overwhelmed, refer to this list and see if you are sticking to your priorities.

1

2

3

4

5

Priorities for Transferees

So far, we have looked at the situation of a new hire who is trying to juggle a new job and employer with the demands of relocation. There is also another possible scenario: that of the transferee. While the transferee does not have to deal with a new employer, her particular challenge is not to lose sight of the work at hand while negotiating and preparing the transfer, and later managing the potential overlap of old and new assignments.

In the early days, when the terms of the transfer are still under discussion and there is little clarity from the employer's side—for some reason transfers are always uncertain until the very last minute—it is important to keep focused on the business and not get caught up in speculation about the future. The best you can do is to make your interests and conditions clear, and then let your manager do her work.

Once your move is confirmed, however, try to avoid getting caught up in "doing-everything-you-wished-you-had-done-but-never-found-the-time-for." It is inevitably tempting to think that no one can do your job as well as you can and to stay involved until the last minute. Keep in mind, though, that from the moment your transfer is confirmed, you will be evaluated based on your new assignment, not your old one. Therefore, your best bet is to get a successor identified as soon as possible, allowing you to hand over your workload and make time for preparing for your relocation. In fact, it is ideal to schedule your handover such that your successor is fully onboard a week or so before you leave, allowing those last days for questions and having a clean cut-off point when you will cease to be available. There is nothing worse than arriving at a new assignment, facing all the challenges discussed earlier in this chapter, with the additional weight of your previous job and successor dragging you down.

○

At this point, you will have made your decision, negotiated your contract, relocated, and settled in at your destination. Now you will finally be able to experience some of your new surroundings: meeting the locals and discovering the country and the culture.

Chapters 4 and 5 will help you on your way by taking a look at the nature of culture and culture shock, and by providing some tools for understanding a different culture.

CULTURE AND CULTURE SHOCK

*Jen left the United States in March 2001, at age 24, when she decided to accept a business reporting job with the **Prague Post**, the Czech Republic's leading English-language newspaper. She set off thinking that living abroad would be like her magical holidays to Europe— only longer. It didn't take much time for her to figure out that fantasy had dominated her expectations. Every single aspect of life—from the kind of toilet paper she could buy, to how to connect a phone line, to getting around and communicating with people—was totally new. All the basic decisions of life, formerly governed by routine, had to be addressed from scratch.*

As a journalist, Jen became aware of her implicit reliance on culture faster than most people. It never occurred to her, back home, how much her life experience played into her ability to do her job or even to survive on a daily basis. In Prague, she suddenly found herself not knowing information others took for granted: from which government agency handles tax collection to what shop sells organic bread. Not only did she have to overcome her discomfort at feeling ignorant and asking seemingly obvious questions, she also had to work twice as hard as her colleagues to get her job done. The extra effort involved took a physical toll. During her first year abroad, she got sick with colds, the flu, and infections far more often than usual.

It took a bit more time for her to begin noticing how profoundly the culture affected the way she did things. On the surface, the communication barrier Jen faced was language related: she didn't speak Czech. Yet even when she was dealing with locals who were proficient in their use of English, she found that her interviews would rarely go as well as she had hoped. The people she talked to were often reserved and curt. Her friendly and chatty manner, so effective back home, seemed only to make matters worse. She soon discovered the impact of history on her host country. Occupation by the Hapsburg Empire from the sixteenth to the nineteenth centuries, followed shortly by the German Reich during World War II, and then the influence of the former Soviet Union had made life difficult for the Czechs and made them suspicious of light-heartedness and wary of answering questions. This was a cultural barrier that went beyond language, and Jen realized that she had to do more than just learn Czech—she had to modify her entire interview approach. She did so by observing her local colleagues, asking questions, and trying until she got it right.

Her initial attempt to make sense of all the differences involved dividing everything into two categories—the way it was at home and the

way it was in Prague. She kept a tally: the beer was dirt cheap and deli-
cious in Prague—plus one for the Czechs. Most stores were closed on
Sundays—minus one for the Czechs. The people were stoic and sometimes
rude—another minus. But when they did open up, they could be authen-
tic and profound—plus two for the Czechs. At some point, though, she
stopped comparing them.

This mental scorecard, she ultimately found, was almost worthless.
One of the best things she did in adjusting to life overseas was to cut out—
or at least dramatically reduce—comparisons to life "back home." She
discovered that by looking at a place and a people through as blank a lens
as she could manage, she opened herself up to their perspective. It wasn't
a question of replacing her way of doing things; rather, she was embrac-
ing a wider range of possibilities, beyond those she already knew. Culture
ceased to be a shock and became an exciting new facet of her life.

Defining Culture

Academia purportedly has over three hundred definitions of *culture*.
Rather than go into a discussion of their relative merits, I have come
up with a simple definition that fits the purposes of this book:
Culture is the sum of characteristic choices made by a group of people.

The first thing to note about culture is that it pertains only to
things that are man-made. The physical environment in its natural
state is not cultural; it would be the same if people did not exist.
However, the characteristic manner in which people relate to their
environment—and to other people—add up to form a culture. For
example, the mountains in Switzerland are not a product of culture,

but the lifestyle that has evolved around them, including the raising of sheep and cattle on the hillsides, the traditions for cheese production, and an attitude of hardiness, is.

Culture as the Product of Choice

Whenever we deal with things created by people, we deal with the products of human choice. Each thing created by a person could equally well have not been created, or it could have been created in a different way. To continue our example, the Swiss could have, historically, chosen to get their sustenance through hunting or berry gathering, but they chose raising cattle as the best solution. Of course, this does not mean that every individual consciously makes such choices. More often than not, children simply emulate the behaviors of their parents and take on the traditional ways of doing things, without realizing that there are alternatives possible.

As early humans strove for survival, they had to make a wide range of choices. On a basic level, they had to figure out what to eat and how to clothe themselves. They also had to address more complex issues, like how to communicate and interact with each other. Finally, on the most abstract level, they had to consider what is good or bad for themselves and for others, and thus decide on a moral system. The particular set of solutions a group adopted on these questions became its culture, and this culture was passed on and improved upon over generations. Since early populations lived in isolation from each other, the choices they made were quite unique, based on their own physical attributes combined with the local geography, climate, and natural resources. Over time, as groups began to interact—warring, more often than not— the dominant one would impose its solutions on the conquered, broadening the sphere of influence not only of its food, clothing, and language, but also its social, legal, and moral system. At this stage, culture ceased to be as intimately linked to the problem of survival in a given region—it became an accepted way of doing things, sometimes detached from local conditions yet still implemented as the legally and socially sanctioned way, embedded in the psyche of the inhabitants. Living in a given culture before the age of mass travel, it was easy to lose sight of the possibility of doing things differently. Even now, mass media is not always sufficient to give a true sense of different cultures. It usually takes travel to another environment to help us realize the full extent to which we have unconsciously adopted the choices and solutions we have grown up with, and that other options are possible on so many levels.

Culture aſ Pertaining to a Group

The next aspect of our definition of culture involves the notion of *group*. Historically, groups were geographically defined, with cultural likeness evolving among people who lived in close proximity, faced similar conditions, and thus made similar choices in their quest for survival. Since then, additional vehicles for the transmission of culture have come into play, and these can override geographical boundaries. One is the extension of political influence: think how Roman culture spread beyond the physical limits of the Italian Peninsula, where it originally evolved. Another is religion, which unites populations under a common moral system and thus guides their choices, even across national boundaries. A final one is language, which allows for the transmission of ideas over time and space: consider how the English language is shaping the evolution of a worldwide business culture, based largely on an Anglo-Saxon philosophy. Nowadays, the cultural groupings of nationality, religion, and language determine our outlook far more than the physical environment we live in.

In addition to the cultural groupings we are born into, as described earlier, we voluntarily adhere to groups whose culture and way of doing things we choose to adopt. The primary one is the workplace—we've all heard the term *company culture*—but a culture also forms around any interest or parameter that people have in common, like a sports club or a seniors' association. Such a group faces common concerns or challenges and adopts more or less consistent attitudes toward them and toward each other, thus creating a group culture.

Culture as the Science and Art of Generalization

The principal challenge that most culture specialists face is contained in a phrase in the previous paragraph: *more or less consistent.* When we say, for example, that French people dress well or that a certain company has an entrepreneurial culture, it doesn't mean that every member in the group behaves this way. It means that there exists a behavior characteristic of the group, even though not all members adopt it. The question then becomes: what conditions must be met for us to be justified in making generalized statements about a group's behavior, that is, about its culture?

The first part of the answer involves sheer statistics. Let's imagine that we want to describe two nationalities, the U.S. Americans and the French, in terms of their attitude toward a basic matter: food. We could say that the Americans generally expend less time and effort preparing food, and prefer fast-food lunches at their desks to lengthy noontime meals at the local bistro. However, this does not mean that Americans never eat elaborate meals, or that French people never eat a quick hamburger.

Figure 4.1 Fast food preferences for U.S. Americans and the French

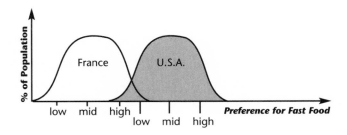

The best way to describe the phenomenon would be as follows: among both the French and the U.S. American populations, there are people with varying degrees of preference for fast food, though overall, the American population has a greater preference for fast food than the French. This is shown graphically in Figure 4.1 (Trompenaars).

That being said, we never hear of countries and cultures described in terms of lengthy lists of statistical comparisons. Often, a few adjectives are enough. We often hear it said that Americans are *businesslike*, because they frequently focus on functionality rather than form. To them, it is important that the body gets nourished, that clothes fit comfortably or, in a business context, that work gets done. By contrast, we can describe the French as *stylish*. To them, it's important that a meal be presented attractively and be tasty, clothes be well cut, and formalities be observed in a business context, even taking precedence over whether a deal gets struck. But how do we go about selecting these particular adjectives? How do we determine that they are in fact significant and telling aspects of the culture?

This is where describing culture becomes an art form rather than a science. It involves tuning into a culture's most fundamental values: those which influence the widest range of behaviors. Returning to our example, both Americans and French will dress elegantly for a formal occasion. However, in the case of the Americans, they likely do so with another end in mind, such as making a good impression in front of potential business contacts. For the French, however, dressing well is typically a matter of principle, of lifestyle, of a form that must be followed for its own sake. In this sense, it is appropriate to describe the French as *well-dressed* or *stylish* because it is very close to their fundamental value of good form. By contrast, dress is not really fundamental to the American culture. Functionality is, and that's why the term *businesslike* is more apt for American culture.

Returning to our definition of culture, the term *characteristic* captures this notion of focusing on the most significant traits of a group: culture is the sum of *characteristic* choices made by a group of people. It reflects both points made above: (a) statistical predominance of a trait, and (b) its relative importance in the value system of the group.

To summarize, people must make a wide variety of choices to survive, ranging from what to eat, through how to communicate, and ending with what to consider good or bad. The characteristic way in which a group of people makes these choices becomes its culture.

Values and Culture

A crucial element of culture, which appears only implicitly in my definition, is the concept of *values*. If we consider culture the characteristic manner in which a group chooses to act, then values are what the group has in common and what allows it to make these consistent, characteristic choices.

Here's how it works. Whenever you are faced with a choice, you must assess your alternatives. To do that, you must have a standard of assessment. Typically, your values are that standard. Let's look at an example: in deciding what to eat, you might think, "A meal at the bistro is a good opportunity to build relationships with my colleagues, but a sandwich at my desk is faster." If your standard of assessment is expediency, then you will choose the sandwich. If your standard is relationships, then you will choose the bistro. Americans by and large value efficiency, so generally they will opt for a sandwich. The French typically value maintaining good form and relationships, so they will likely head to the bistro.

Thus, in any attempt to decipher a culture, you need to identify the values that guide it. If you simply look at all the phenomena visible on the surface, you may get the impression of an infinite number of differences that you can't possibly list or group. As a European arriving in America, you might be struck by the fact that Americans walk around with coffee in travel mugs, have oversize fridges in their houses, and show up at work in jeans. The list of things that surprise you in this way could go on and on. However, you could account for much of this and capture it by identifying an underlying value that gives rise to all of these, that is, *efficiency*. Having coffee while on the go is more efficient than sitting down for half an hour. A large fridge allows for a large shopping trip once a week, instead of purchasing fresh food daily—again, it is more efficient. At work, what matters is getting the job done, not appearance. If jeans allow employees to feel comfortable and work more efficiently, then they are welcome in the workplace.

In this sense, identifying the values that are at the heart of a culture allows us to see the inner logic guiding all the phenomena we encounter on the surface (we will look at how to identify these values in the next chapter). One metaphor that has been widely used, and which remains helpful in describing the relationship of values to culture, is that of an iceberg, shown in Figure 4.2. Here we see that items on the surface represent the tangible—the audible and visible—aspects of culture, and the part under water symbolizes the intangible aspects—the values.

Figure 4.2 The tangible and intangible aspects of culture

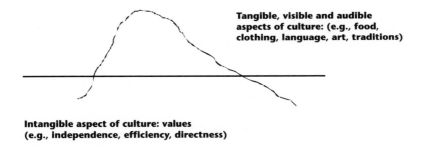

Tangible, visible and audible aspects of culture: (e.g., food, clothing, language, art, traditions)

Intangible aspect of culture: values (e.g., independence, efficiency, directness)

Culture ∫hock

Thus far, we've defined culture as the characteristic way of doing things chosen by a group of people. We've further said that, as a new generation growing up within a certain culture, you might not be aware that your way of doing things is in fact the result of choice, or that alternate ways are possible. Culture is as natural a background to you as the air you breathe.

Culture shock occurs when you are taken out of your usual environment and the change makes you aware of how much you assume in your daily behavior, in the same way that the absence of air would make you conscious of your need to breathe. Changes in your cultural setting "shock" you for several reasons:

1. *They challenge what you take for granted and shake your established habits.* You may have always eaten your main meal of the day at 6:00 P.M. and prepared it yourself. Suddenly you find yourself in a country where the main meal is eaten during the early afternoon and prepared by servants. You may actually prefer the new arrangement, but it still represents a change, and accumulation of changes that come with relocation can be very unsettling.

2. *They may not be immediately apparent.* Material things, like dress, and some aspects of etiquette, like bowing instead of shaking hands, are pretty easy to pin down as cultural phenomena. But you may consider having dinner guests show up an hour late particular to them and simply rude, while it might be a case of a wider-spread and acceptable practice. It takes time and context to be able to assess this, and in the interim you may feel disoriented.

3. *They can have unexpectedly far-reaching consequences.* Moving from north to south, you probably expect some difference in the way time is perceived, but you may not expect in how many ways this will affect your life: from something simple like overcooking dinner because your guests don't show up on time, through having to adapt your usual way of scheduling a project to allow for the inevitable *mañana* attitude, and even with the time you suddenly have to spend on building relationships. As you realize all the implications of what seemed a minor difference, you may feel overwhelmed at the extent of adaptation required.

4. *Most importantly, they call upon you to re-evaluate.* As discussed earlier, a large part of culture involves choice and values. As humans, we choose our course of action because it seems the best possible under the circumstances, because we believe it to be right according to our standards or values. When you move to another country, the standards may be different, and behavior you considered to be right may suddenly be considered inappropriate, or even punishable. Considering again the example of a move from north to south, when your dinner guests arrive one hour late, by your northern standards of punctuality they are rude, but by their standards they are within the norm. So this opens the question: Which standards do you use when judging others? And for your own actions?

If you think about it, as a GenXpat you have probably taken twenty to thirty years to acquire your culture, that is, your way of dealing with material and moral questions. Some of it may have been conscious—you may have actually thought about what you prefer to eat for breakfast or whether democracy is a good social system—but you probably absorbed a tremendous amount implicitly. Chances are that you do not even realize you usually stand on the right side of an escalator and walk up or down on the left side. You simply do it.

A cultural change throws you into an environment where you can no longer rely on the habits and rules that you implicitly call upon at home. It requires you to make conscious choices, in a very short span of time, on questions that took you a lifetime to address, either deliberately or by imitating those around you.

These huge adjustments, and the emotions of uncertainty and frustration accompanying them, make up culture shock. Going though it successfully can be very rewarding, though, as you end up with a more integrated and consciously held outlook on the world, which results in greater self-confidence and maturity.

It is important to note that culture shock often is compounded by homesickness, and this distinct phenomenon can occur even within your own culture. Homesickness involves missing the predictability of home, as well as the family, friendships, and support networks that go with it (more on this in Chapter 6).

How Do We Experience Culture Shock?

In real life we don't experience culture shock as a definition or even as a rational dissection like the preceding one. Rather, we go through a series of emotional reactions, first identified as five distinct phases by the anthropologist Kalvero Oberg.

1. *Honeymoon.* Imagine that your relocation takes you to a place that seems attractive and exotic to you: transferring from cold and rainy Geneva to sunny Israel or from an impoverished dictatorship to the United States, the land of opportunity. Initially, everything seems wonderful. Living near the Tel Aviv beaches is a treat, as is the bustling nightlife. Or, in the other scenario, you're busy savoring the full extent of personal freedom available in the United States. Emotionally you are riding on high;

intellectually you perceive all the advantages of the host country, while glossing over any differences as minor and superficial. (Note: For some, especially those not looking forward to their destination, the Honeymoon phase may not occur.)

2. *Rejection.* After a period of days or months, cracks begin to appear in the initially polished surface of your experience. In Tel Aviv, the constant heat begins to wear you down, as does the incessant noise and activity. You experience a rising irritation with your surroundings. As an immigrant to the United States, you may begin to feel the weight of responsibility that comes with freedom, such as planning for illness and retirement. Emotionally, this can mean insecurity and stress. Intellectually, in this phase you focus on the negatives of your situation. In terms of the discussion in the previous section, you're in the process of discovering the full and far-reaching implications of cultural differences as you become aware of the degree to which you need to adapt and yet instinctively resist the change.

3. *Regression.* In some but not necessarily all cases, resisting the change may lead you into a period of severe rejection of your new surroundings, during which you want to have as little as possible to do with your host country. At the same time, you're likely to idealize your home and seek out familiar foods, music, movies, and especially other expats of your nationality with whom you can share your complaints. Emotionally, this phase is very close to depression, while intellectually it's a form of denial. You sense that need to adapt and reassess the way you do things, but you're subconsciously afraid to do so. It may be that learning about your new surroundings means admitting that you don't know how things are done or that you need to question some of your basic assumptions—and this is hard to do as an adult, especially if you've been sent abroad because you are very accomplished.

4. *Recovery.* At this stage, you start taking a balanced view of things. Yes, Tel Aviv is hot and busy, but you can get away for a weekend to the north and enjoy the delicious calm and cool of mountains and nature. As an immigrant, you become more familiar with the U.S. system and learn to enjoy your freedom and manage it effectively. Emotionally, you begin feeling at ease in your new surroundings during this phase. Intellectually, you've gained enough context to correctly interpret what's going on (at least most of the time), and you've decided which aspects and values of the host country you want to adopt while there, which ones are so sound that you might even carry them over when you return home, and which ones you really cannot appreciate but have found ways to deal with.

5. *Reverse culture shock.* You have adjusted your way of doing things and values to life abroad. What do you think happens when you get home? Of course—you perceive things differently than you did before you left, requiring a period of readjustment upon your return. I won't go into any more detail at this point, because I devote all of Chapter 11 to this phase.

Each of these five phases is experienced to a lesser or greater degree depending on the person and the culture at hand. Still, these give a good sense of what you might expect to have to cope with.

Dealing with Culture Shock

Three things determine how well you deal with culture shock: (1) your ability to cope with change, including all the superficial differences you'll encounter abroad (different foods, clothing, climate, and so on), (2) your ability to figure out the more profound value differences at play, and (3) your ability to deal with homesickness. We'll look at strategies to improve your proficiency with each of these.

In his book *Managing Transitions*, William Bridges differentiates between *change*, which is external and immediate, and *transition*, which is the individual's reaction to change and often takes time. Transitions involve progressively letting go of the familiar and opening ourselves to new ways of doing things and to methods at which we may not be experts, which means we face the increased possibility of making a mistake (and who wants to make mistakes?). So how can we make transitions as smooth as possible?

● *Keep your objectives in mind.* When you're in an unfamiliar situation and there's a greater risk of failure, try to think of what got you there in the first place. After all, there must have been some perceived advantages driving your decision! You can use these as a carrot to give you the extra courage or motivation you need. If you took the time to write down your objectives for your relocation in Chapter 1, you'll probably find this list very useful when facing the heat of culture shock, wondering why in hell you decided to leave the comforts of home.

○ *Try to be balanced and realistic.* When making your decision to move, try to find out and factor in all the good and bad aspects of both your home and destination, so that you'll have an idea beforehand of what you will be gaining—and what you will be giving up. Remember: unexpected bad news is far worse than bad news you've had time to prepare for.

○ *Be ready to try new things, make mistakes, and admit that you don't know—it's all part of learning.* One of the best anecdotes related to this came from one of my bosses. "What do you think makes the difference between a vice president and the CEO of a company?" he asked. "The VP, at some point, has decided that he has gained all the knowledge he needs, while the CEO has never stopped looking for gaps in his knowledge, asking questions, trying stuff, making mistakes, and learning. That's what put him ahead of everyone else."

The remaining two skills required to deal effectively with culture shock are the ability to identify and address value differences and the ability deal with homesickness. We will look at each one in turn in the upcoming chapters.

IDENTIFYING AND WORKING WITH CULTURAL DIFFERENCES

5

Nick, 29, began his career in the wine industry in British Columbia, first as a sommelier and later by working for a local wine importer. Two years ago, he joined a French winery as its export consultant for the U.S. and Canadian markets. His work involves spending almost half a year in France and collaborating closely with the French family that has owned the company for decades, as well as with the customers who visit the vineyards.

"When I first started to work for the Chancel family, I would address the owner as Jean-Louis or Jean. No one ever made mention of this or tried to correct me but, as time went on, I realized that I, the Canadian, was the only one to do so, even among those who had worked for the Chancels for over 10 years. Now, 18 months later, I address

him as Monsieur Chancel. It's not that I was told to act in one way or the other; I simply didn't want to stand out. I believe it is proper to stand out in the workplace, but only when it's for superlative performance, original ideas, or strength of character. Standing out because I am new, a foreigner, or because I speak to the boss with what can appear to be a lack of respect isn't what I had in mind.

"Then there was the question of dress. U.S. Americans and Canadians, and especially those from the West Coast, are extremely casual in their business attire. To meet a German on a Sunday for a tour of the vineyards in light rain you'll need to wear a blazer, tie, and gum- boots. France isn't quite as formal, but still far more so than the Napa Valley, for example. Over time, I learned to adapt my dress to reflect what is customary in the region. This doesn't mean that, when I travel from Hamburg to Houston, I lose my personal style, or that I exchange an Armani tie and shoes for a bolo tie and cowboy boots. I will, how- ever, choose a suit with a less formal color and weight, and pair it with a simple shirt and no tie. This allows my appearance to be a neutral background, rather than a cause for comment, and keeps the focus on the work at hand.

"I also noticed that relationships outside of work are different. Back home, I might talk to my colleagues about the latest crazy night out on the town, the girls we danced with, and the booze we drank. This raised some eyebrows in France, where travel, food, soccer, and cycling are the more common topics of conversation. Romantic situations are referred to obliquely, if at all. Also, I initially misinterpreted the high level of physical interaction between men as signifying something more. I am used to keeping a foot or two of space between my colleagues and myself. My Italian buddies would link arms with me as we walked down the

street, kiss hello, even step out on the dance floor together. Eventually, I learned to accept this as normal. How does this relate to business? By adapting to the local standard of behavior, you end up with a more natural, comfortable interaction, and this ultimately strengthens the relationship you have with your customers and suppliers—and sales is 99 percent relationship."

Seven Factors for Analyzing Culture

As we discussed in the previous chapter, it is very important to discover the values that the members of a given culture hold, as these are the key to understanding, interpreting, and anticipating the people's behavior. Management researchers and anthropologists have developed a number of frameworks in an attempt to capture the intangible aspects of culture and to make cultural comparisons possible. I have drawn on the work of Geert Hofstede (*www.geert-hofstede.com*), Fons Trompenaars (*www.trompenaars.net/index1.html*), and Edward T. Hall to provide you with seven factors that shape the way people think and act.

Each factor is defined in terms of two opposite attitudes, but the overall factor allows for a whole range of interim behaviors. When I have listed a country or region as representative of a certain attitude, it is because studies show the attitude to be more common there, but remember that there may be significant cultural variations even within one country, especially when dealing with unique population subgroups such as the French in Canada, American companies in China, urban versus rural populations, upper versus lower class, and so on. Keep in mind, though, that these factors are meant only as a starting point for diagnosing your home and host country cultures and as a tool to facilitate your cultural understanding. They are not, however, a basis for prejudging any country or individual. These factors are

1. Personal Identity
2. Power Differential
3. Attitude to Change
4. Notions of Time
5. Communication Style
6. Etiquette
7. Emotional Expression

The following sections describe these in detail.

• *Personal Identity*

One factor that shapes a culture is how people view themselves, or personal identity. Do they see themselves primarily as independent individuals or as part of a group? In an individualistic workplace, people generally believe in personal initiative, decision-making, and responsibility, and thus they expect to be singled out for their professional contributions. Socially, they value independence and privacy, which often means that they live alone or with their immediate families. In more group-oriented societies, the work environment tends to be more collaborative, decisions are made in consultation with others, and recognition is given to the group as a whole. Maintaining relationships is very important and can take precedence over business or personal needs. Extended families often live together or in close proximity. Figure 5.1 shows the personal identity continuum and countries or regions that are representative of either end, listed in descending order of importance (so the United States is the most individualistic, the Commonwealth is a little less, and so on). You can see that Latin America and Asia are more representative of group-oriented cultures.

Figure 5.1 Personal identity continuum

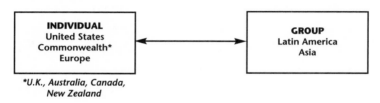

What kinds of conflicts can occur between people who are at opposite ends of this continuum? If you have an individual orientation, chances are that you feel comfortable working independently, arriving at your own conclusions, and making recommendations based on your own judgment. Your group-oriented colleagues may perceive this as moving ahead too quickly without due consultation, pushing yourself forward, and being competitive or insensitive. To work more effectively with them, you might find it useful to take the time and get their input, even if you have sole responsibility in a certain area. If you have a group-oriented manager who evaluates you, keep in mind that he views your success as primarily a function of your team's success.

If you have a group orientation, chances are that you feel comfortable arriving at conclusions through discussion and building agreement over time, so that when the decision point occurs there is already a pre-aligned consensus within your group. In an individually oriented environment, you may be seen as showing little personal initiative, having slow or unclear decision-making processes, and getting tied down with irrelevant interpersonal considerations. When dealing with individually oriented coworkers, do not hesitate to voice your ideas, even if they are not consistent with those of the group. If you need to pre-align with superiors back home, let your colleagues know what is going on and why, so they do not think you are stalling. Finally, if you have an individually oriented manager assessing you, remember that he or she is looking for signs of your contribution—"I did"—rather than the group's work as a whole—"we did"—so speak up!

• *Power Differential*
Another factor that defines a culture is the degree of power differential (PD) between members of a society. In societies with a low PD, social and corporate hierarchies are fairly flat and flexible. This means that people can earn their way to positions of power based on their ability to fulfill a certain mandate. Their authority is limited to that mandate and they remain equal to other people in the eyes of the law. In societies with a high PD, only people with a certain family background, education, gender, or level of

seniority can attain positions of power, which creates a stratified society that cannot be overcome by merit alone. Also, not all citizens of these societies necessarily have the same legal rights.

In a workplace with low PD, subordinates tend to take initiative and embrace responsibility because good performance is the main factor determining their progress in the organization. Managers typically welcome debate and usually happily delegate work because it frees up their time for other tasks. In companies with a high PD, positions of power are not open to everyone and employees are not encouraged to overstep their responsibilities. Figure 5.2 provides some examples of countries at either end of the power differential continuum.

Figure 5.2 Power differential continuum

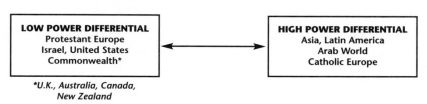

What kinds of conflicts can occur between people who come from opposite ends of the continuum? If you come from a background with low PD, you may find that you often question the status quo in search of the best solutions. If you find yourself in a country with a strict hierarchy, your colleagues may perceive you as unnecessarily challenging the system, with potentially bad consequences for them, and your superiors may find you disrespectful or even threatening. You might like to tread very lightly, because in these countries you can be penalized for not following procedures or showing respect—even if you know that you are in the right.

If you come from a country with high PD, you likely feel it is best to follow proper processes and to refer unusual cases to your superior. In countries where low PD is prevalent, this approach may be perceived as bureaucratic or unoriginal and as attempting to avoid responsibility. More often than not, a boss with low PD will consider it better for you to take action, even if it means making a mistake, than to take no action at all. It is important to remember that in countries with low PD, people consider themselves fundamentally equal, so it is always better to ask politely rather than place demands on subordinates, assistants, and household help.

• *Attitude to Change*

The degree to which people willingly embrace uncertainty or change characterizes another cultural attitude. In some societies, primarily those influenced by Protestantism, people believe that they can shape their future through their own actions. They tend to be more comfortable with novel, risky, or ambiguous situations because they feel that they can manage such situations in their own favor. Interestingly, fatalism can sometimes also mean openness to risk; this is more visible in the Asian world. Other cultures feel that the individual is only a small part of a larger society or tradition and that he has little influence on the way things are done, so it is best for him if he goes with the flow. He feels comfortable with time-honored ways of doing things and tends to avoid change. Figure 5.3 captures the countries and regions that are representative of these opposite beliefs.

Figure 5.3 Attitude to change continuum

What kinds of conflicts can occur? If you come from a culture that embraces change, you might find yourself eagerly trying new things and taking risks in the pursuit of a better future. In a more traditional environment, your actions may be perceived as impetuous and unpredictable, possibly even threatening. You might find it helpful to proceed more slowly when introducing new ideas to peers or subordinates, taking the time to provide background information, answer questions, and discuss implications. If you learn that "things aren't done that way here," ask how they *do* get done: traditional societies often have ways of indirectly circumventing the system that may seem complicated to you, but are actually the most direct route to results.

If you come from a traditional culture, you likely place value on proven methods of doing things. In a fast-changing society, you may be perceived as passive, predictable, and not driving innovation. It might help you to consider that while you focus on what can be lost by doing something new, your colleagues believe they can only achieve success by attempting something new and that maintaining the status quo inherently leads to loss.

• Notions of Time

Another factor that distinguishes a culture is its notion of time. In some societies time is rigid: objectives must be reached within a specified time and tasks are scheduled accordingly. The logic is that getting more done in a given time frame leads to increased earnings (time is money), so people tend to be in a rush to meet deadlines and they value punctuality. This attitude extends to the social sphere, where people plan gatherings in advance and hosts expect guests to show up on time. In other cultures, people consider the quality of the time spent as more important than the quantity of things that get done. Thus work can be interrupted to help a colleague or a friend. Deadlines and schedules tend to be fluid. At social events, guests may arrive much later than the scheduled time and family and friends usually welcome impromptu visits. Figure 5.4 illustrates that notions of time are more rigid in Germanic countries, such as Germany, Austria, and Switzerland, and in the United States, while time is more fluid in the Catholic European countries, like France, Belgium, or Italy, as well as Latin America and Japan.

Figure 5.4 Attitude to time continuum

TIME IS RIGID	TIME IS FLUID
Germanic Countries*	Catholic Europe
United States	Latin America
Commonwealth†	Japan

*Germany, Austria, Switzerland
†U.K., Australia, Canada, New Zealand

What kinds of conflicts can occur? If you come from a culture where time is rigid, you may have a tendency to save time by getting straight down to business during meetings and to regularly follow up on the progress of a project to make sure it is on track. If you move to a country where time is fluid, you may be seen as cold or insensitive to social niceties, as well as pushy and impatient. Try not to get frustrated by the delays; rather, take the time to enjoy the relationship-building process. Paradoxically, this gets things accomplished faster: remember that people will interrupt their work to help a friend.

If you come from a country where time is fluid, you will likely want to get to know people before discussing business, and building a good relationship will take precedence over meeting a deadline. When working with people who view time as rigid, your approach may seem inefficient and your flexible attitude to deadlines may appear undependable. It is important not to be offended when your colleagues proceed straight to business; their apparent lack of interest is not a testimony to their opinion of you; rather, they are saving social interaction for a time when the work is done. You might like to try to match their style during business meetings and build relationships when they do: at lunch or after work. With regard to deadlines, you will appear more professional by setting a more distant date for a project and meeting it than by promising something sooner and not delivering it.

• *Communication Style*
One more factor that shapes a culture is the preferred way of communication, or the communication style. In some countries,

importance is placed on delivering a message as explicitly and directly as possible, even if it involves a refusal, bad news, or negative feedback. People do not consider such communication offensive; rather, the recipient appreciates it because it allows him or her to take corrective measures—hence the saying "feedback is a gift." In other cultures, conveyance of bad news or feedback tends to be more indirect or implicit, and may be achieved by omission, hints, or even intermediaries, to allow the recipient to save face. These cultures avoid direct refusals out of concern for damaging the harmonious functioning of a group or relationship. As you can see in Figure 5.5, the United States, Australia, Canada, and New Zealand tend to prefer direct communication, while people in Asia and Latin America convey their messages less explicitly.

Figure 5.5 Communication style continuum

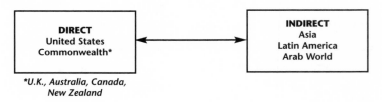

What kinds of conflicts can occur? If you are used to conveying your messages directly, you may actually be hurtful, insulting, or embarrassing to your colleagues accustomed to indirect communication. You may be perceived as insensitive, disrespectful, or as having poor manners. Communicating effectively in these circumstances can be very tricky, because the proper means of delivery are culturally coded and you are not used to giving or receiving this particular code. Your best bet is to begin by observing and listening—a lot. If someone wants to tell you something and you listen long enough, the point will eventually come across. This can be an opportunity to see the techniques people use to convey difficult messages. In general, though, you might find it useful to avoid saying outright that something is bad or wrong, and try to focus on how things can be improved instead. If you are unsure how to interpret or communicate something, consider asking one of your local peers to advise you.

If you prefer to communicate indirectly and you are dealing with people who favor directness, you may come across as unclear, unnecessarily complicating things, or even harboring a hidden agenda. If you convey your message through someone else, you could be seen as disloyal or backstabbing. It may help you to consider that explicit communicators actually value your input as long as you give it to them directly, face-to-face. They prefer to hear it from you so that they can fix whatever is wrong—before anyone else learns about it. This is one reason why it is not a good idea to ask a peer to transmit the information.

• Etiquette

Another factor that defines a culture is the importance attached to etiquette and protocol. In informal societies, job performance and moral uprightness matter most, while titles, family background, and outward appearance take second place. People tend to be on a first-name basis, and there are fewer explicit rules dictating social conduct, such as "you must stand in the presence of elders" or "men shouldn't wear hats indoors." It is, however, very important to be respectful to all people, regardless of social background. In formal societies, observing proper etiquette is at least as important as job performance and moral uprightness. Explicit rules exist concerning use of titles, precedence, proper attire, table manners, appropriate small talk, and so on. Only a narrow group of close friends will be asked to move to a first-name basis and allowed more informality. Figure 5.6 gives you an idea of where informality and formality prevail respectively.

Figure 5.6 The etiquette continuum

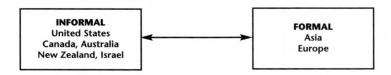

What kinds of conflicts can occur? If you are used to informal interaction, you may not be aware of all the rules in your host country, or you may discount them as too complicated or as irrelevant. In some cases, your disregard may be insulting to your more formal peers, or it may make you appear as disrespectful or ill-bred and close the avenue for further interaction. On the other hand, some more formally oriented people may take your use of first names to be the sign of a deeper friendship, and may then consider you hypocritical for showing these signs and yet remaining at the level of a casual acquaintance. To be successful in a formal environment, remember that while knowing the social rules is not a substitute for having something to say, it will help you gain access to your audience and allow your messages to be heard. So do take the time to learn the titles and roles of your more formal colleagues and find out what is considered appropriate dress and behavior.

If you are used to formal interaction, you may be tempted to transpose the rules of your home country to an informal environment. This can backfire, though. By continuing to use titles when speaking to your superiors, for example, you may be perceived as trying to gain favor, as being very stiff and conformist, or even as too shy or too elitist to use first names and be "one of the gang." You may also be considered superficial for attaching so much importance to dress and form, and people might wonder if you are doing it to hide your inability to do your job. One way you can avoid these complications is by going ahead and using first names and to approximately match the degree of formality of your colleagues' clothing. That being said, you do not need to be friendlier than you actually feel. If you are not comfortable with backslapping and joking around with your bosses, do not do it, as it will appear false.

• Emotional Expression

The final factor affecting culture, at least in this list, is the degree and means in which people express emotions. Some societies consider it best to refrain from outwardly revealing thoughts and emotions, be it through facial expressions, bodily gestures, or an emotional tone of voice. In other cultures, outward expressions of emotions are perfectly acceptable, making it okay to hug and kiss colleagues and friends as a sign of welcome, or to show excitement, approval, or disagreement through facial expressions and voice modulation. As shown in Figure 5.7, some of the more reserved countries or regions include Japan, China, and Northern Europe, while Latin America and the Arab world tend to be more affective.

Figure 5.7 The emotional expression continuum

What kinds of conflicts can occur? If you tend to be reserved, your affective colleagues may view you as cold, stiff, or unapproachable. They may also think that you do not like them or consider yourself superior. If you tend to be emotional, your more reserved coworkers may perceive you as immature, unprofessional, or even out of control. They may feel overwhelmed by the intensity of your reactions, both positive and negative. While it may feel unnatural, you do not have much choice, in either case, other than to try to match your colleagues' behavior as much as you can without compromising your personality. If you sense a big disparity between the way you and your colleagues express emotions, you might like to ask someone you feel comfortable with to let you know which of your behaviors stand out the most or are most likely to cause offense. The very fact that you asked may circulate in the organization and help soften your image.

Using the Factors to Diagnose a Culture

Let us go back to Nick's story at the beginning of this chapter and look at how knowledge of these seven cultural factors could have helped him anticipate some of the cultural differences he encountered. To begin with, the factors would have suggested to him that the French are likely to have a higher power differential and be more formal and traditional than Canadians. They also tend to be more affective.

Armed with this information, Nick could have broken things down further. Since higher PD usually means that the relationship between superiors and subordinates involves gestures of respect, Nick could have made a mental note to inquire about suitable ways of addressing and dealing with his boss. Formality and respect for tradition typically require that people remain within a range of appropriate behavior, including unwritten rules around dress code and suitable topics of conversation. Again, knowing that there would be unfamiliar procedures to follow, Nick could have planned to seek advice, either by speaking to other people or reading up on the subject. Finally, affective cultures are more likely to accept physical interaction among colleagues, and knowing this could have spared Nick some worries!

All in all, knowledge of the cultural factors can help direct some of your preparatory questions as you head abroad. It can also enable you to correctly interpret behaviors that may be otherwise surprising or shocking. So it is worth taking a minute to situate your home and host cultures with respect to the seven cultural factors and to consider what this can mean in practical terms. Use Figure 5.8 to mark the countries' relative positions. If you are unsure where your destination fits in, try consulting the Hofstede and Trompenaars websites or talk to expats of your nationality who already live there.

Figure 5.8 Comparing your home and host countries

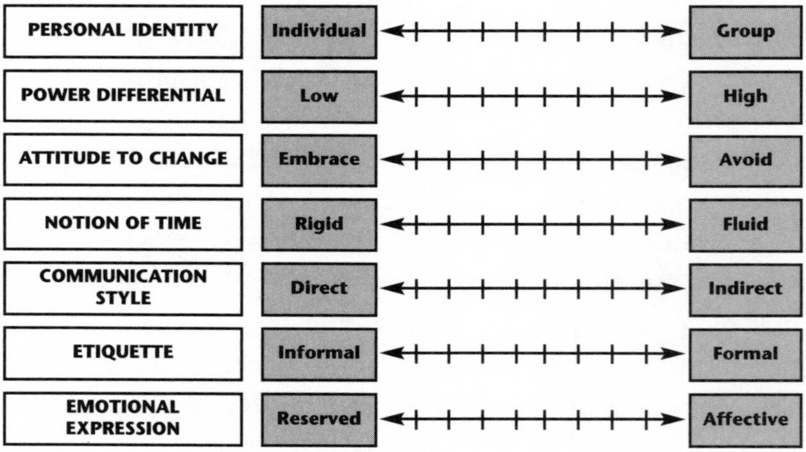

PERSONAL IDENTITY	Individual	←─┼─┼─┼─┼─┼─┼─┼─┼─→	Group
POWER DIFFERENTIAL	Low	←─┼─┼─┼─┼─┼─┼─┼─┼─→	High
ATTITUDE TO CHANGE	Embrace	←─┼─┼─┼─┼─┼─┼─┼─┼─→	Avoid
NOTION OF TIME	Rigid	←─┼─┼─┼─┼─┼─┼─┼─┼─→	Fluid
COMMUNICATION STYLE	Direct	←─┼─┼─┼─┼─┼─┼─┼─┼─→	Indirect
ETIQUETTE	Informal	←─┼─┼─┼─┼─┼─┼─┼─┼─→	Formal
EMOTIONAL EXPRESSION	Reserved	←─┼─┼─┼─┼─┼─┼─┼─┼─→	Affective

Appropriate Level of Cultural Adaptation

A final point to consider about cultural adaptation is the degree to which it is necessary and appropriate to modify your behavior. The primary purpose of cultural adaptation is to increase your effectiveness at achieving professional and personal goals in a foreign context. As Nick discovered, using correct titles, dressing appropriately, and being open to more affective behavior allowed him to build the relationships he needed to get his job done.

That being said, the purpose of cultural adaptation is *not* to become one of the locals. *Going native*, as this is called, and adapting to the local values and customs at the expense of your own can ultimately be very damaging to your sense of identity. It often starts because you are somehow disillusioned with your own culture—or you simply believe that another culture is better—and you wish to take on another way of being. As you attempt to substitute a new cultural context and values for the ones you grew up with, you may discover that the impact is far broader than what you imagined, and that perhaps you cannot give up your original outlook in some areas. There is also the question of personal history. While you may like to think that you started anew when you changed cultural contexts, the fact remains that your personal history remains in your home country. Even if you do not mind not having your home-country history around you, you might discover that not having a personal history in the hostcountry becomes a challenge when trying to relate to the locals, who all share this bond. The almost inevitable result is something of an identity crisis, where you find yourself no longer identifying with home, but also never quite integrating with the locals in the host country. It also makes it difficult for the locals to situate you in their own minds, since you are neither a total foreigner nor entirely a local.

○

The only way to build a healthy intercultural relationship is to remain true to your identity while showing respect and understanding of the local culture. The challenge, of course, lies in finding this line: which aspects of your beliefs and behavior are core to your identity and cannot be changed, and which ones are optional. There is no right answer to this; most people get a sense for what works through experience.

KEEPING IN TOUCH

6

Ask any expat who has been away for more than a couple of years how many friends he or she has kept in touch with back home. Often, you will learn, it's no more than a handful.

I brought this up one night over dinner with Jesse, 28, a native Vancouverite who had recently come home. He had left six years ago to pursue a career in banking. He joined the RBC Financial Group in Toronto, did a stint for them in the Big Apple, and then topped things off with an MBA at INSEAD. Now he was back in Vancouver—perhaps to stay— and was facing the challenge of reconnecting with friends and acquaintances.

He explained that he had never been part of one fixed group. He preferred the variety of having a number of differ- ent social circles and he prided himself on not mixing friends, spending time with each person individually. His tailored approach had trained him to be proactive in matters of keeping in touch even before he left, yet even he was surprised at how challenging it was to maintain bonds over distance. "Since I left," he told me, "aside from family members, only two of my West Coast friends have come to visit me. Six years, two friends."

Jesse found trips home only a little more conducive to fueling deep friendships. He would typically fly home twice a year, once during the summer and once at Christmas. Each time, his week's holiday would be booked like a tour schedule. Two dinners a night weren't uncommon. While it was good to hear his friends' news, not everyone could relate to his experiences, making the exchanges only partly satisfying.

As he considered the question of what it takes to maintain friendships over distance, Jesse realized that a large part of his social life at home survived thanks to his friend Dave. Dave was a hockey and drinking buddy from their university days, a good friend, but not someone Jesse had expected to keep in touch with. So it was somewhat to Jesse's surprise that they talked on the phone periodically, e-mailed occasionally, and, most importantly, Dave became the first person Jesse contacted when he came into town. Dave organized ski trips for each New Year's Eve, and it became a joke between them that Jesse was always the first to sign up among a group of notoriously noncommitting friends: he booked a spot for the next year's trip before even leaving the mountain! Beyond that, Dave made it a point to know when Jesse was coming home and made sure he was invited to all the parties, camping trips, and spontaneous drinking nights. Dave was a connector.

What allowed their friendship to last? On one level, Dave and Jesse had a shared history from their university days and a tight bond from having played hockey together. They also had a good day-to-day connection thanks to the fact that they both worked in finance, got their MBAs, and completed their CFAs (Chartered Financial Analyst exams) at the same time. What saved them from dreary factual exchanges was the difference in their respective outlooks on life: Dave is an idea guy, often racing after the next big thing, while Jesse is somewhat more conservative and a bit of a self-confessed plodder when it comes to work. The fact that they faced similar challenges at the same time, yet approached them from different points of view, allowed them to connect and to learn from each other and build a rich relationship.

Still, friendships can't be boiled down to a recipe of calls, e-mails, and tightly scheduled trips home. Last year, Jesse decided at the last minute to hop on an eleven-hour flight home on his three-day October break to attend his friend Steph's wedding. The groom was one of the hockey buddies and a mutual friend of Jesse and Dave's. The look of pleasure on Steph's face as Jesse showed up among the guests, unannounced, completing the circle of friends, more than justified the travel and expense. The gesture went beyond the wedding itself; it validated the effort they had all put into keeping their friendship alive and sealed the bonds for years to come.

Thus far, we have seen that relocation for professional reasons involves many challenges: juggling an overwhelming number of priorities, learning to manage change, and adapting to a new culture. These are the basics for surviving abroad. Gaining a sense of balance and fulfillment, however, comes from building a satisfying personal life. This includes managing homesickness, learning how to keep in touch with family and friends who have stayed behind, and learning how to create new relationships at destination. Over the next two chapters, we will look at strategies that can help you in all these respects.

Homesickness

Homesickess manifests itself as a desperate longing for home. For some, the focus is on things, including familiar spaces, buildings, geography, and food. For others it is on the people who have stayed behind. It milder cases, it can be just an undercurrent: while you feel that your destination is exotic and the people are friendly, nothing is quite as satisfying as it would be if your close friends were there to appreciate it. In more acute cases, the destination loses all charm. You may be overcome by a resentment of your new surroundings and of the job that has taken you away from home. You may not even be interested in looking at your new environment because you are so busy focusing on home.

One GenXpat recalls an American couple who moved to France. For the duration of their posting, the couple complained about how everything was unsatisfactory when compared to the United States, including the poor customer service, the dirty streets, and the cramped urban areas. Finally, after two years, they went home. No one was more surprised than their French co-workers when they received an e-mail a year later, asking about possible job openings. It turned out that the couple had in fact grown to like France, and that the United States was not the idyllic place they had made it out to be.

Allowing yourself to miss home—or, in the case of serial GenXpats, all the places you have lived in before—can positively drive you crazy. Worse, it can take you away from living and enjoying the present moment, while you dwell on everything you have left behind. This does not mean that you should never be homesick. While abroad, you can occasionally go buy your favorite food at your national food store or start up a conversation with a fellow expat you run across on the street. Sometimes you can pick up the phone and randomly call friends back home, regardless of the expense. However, most of the time it makes sense to focus on the life at destination as the only one available. It is really an effort to live in the present, thinking about the opportunities at hand, rather than in the past or the future. The secret to happiness abroad, and perhaps in general, is wanting what you have, rather than missing what you have not got.

If, for whatever reason, you cannot bring yourself to appreciate your new environment, then you might like to revisit your objectives for the relocation. Do they still hold as valid, given the intensity of your dissatisfaction with life at destination? Or are you so homesick that your new job and/or promotion are just not worth it? If you are constantly unhappy over six months to a year, then it makes sense to acknowledge that and go home. Even if you are concerned that it may look bad professionally, your unhappiness will eventually transpire into your work and could end up looking worse than simply recognizing that things are not working and finding a way to go home.

In most cases, however, homesickness is most acute a few months into the move, and then tends to fade. It is best managed by keeping a good open line of communication with family and friends who have stayed at home, that is, using their support to thrive in your life abroad. Keeping in touch should not mean trying to live at home vicariously, through your friends. That would fall right into the category of acute homesickness!

The Importance of Keeping in Touch

Most of us, at some point, have dreamed of going away and starting over. We fantasized about building friendships from scratch, uncluttered by any established image or reputation, past mistakes, or complex emotional demands. Indeed, upon arriving in a new place, you can quickly make a large circle of acquaintances, as people are curious about you and your background. The introductory chitchat puts you in the center of attention, the dinners and parties are entertaining.

Just as you may be congratulating yourself on having made the transition so successfully, you may find things slowing down. Introductions will have been made, information exchanged, and people—especially the locals—will be settling back into the social routines they had before you arrived. Since most people already have a set of close friends who satisfy their emotional needs and fill their schedules, it is quite unusual for them to adopt a newcomer deep into the fold. Another challenge in making this connection can be the language and cultural barrier. It may simply require more effort on their part to include you, and you may not get the same sense of connection that you might with someone who shares your history and cultural references, like your favorite sports team or TV show. Suddenly, the familiarity of long-standing relationships you had with your friends and family at home may seem very appealing. For all their complexity, they carry the benefit of a shared history and the acceptance of your strengths and weaknesses; they are a part of your identity. No matter how tempting it may be to leave everything behind, or to simply get caught up in all the excitement of going away, it is nevertheless vital to nurture these relationships. They will often be the ones that will carry you through the darker days of expatriation.

Saying Good-bye

Keeping in touch should ideally begin even before you head off to your destination. I know that it may be hard to make the time for proper good-byes amid all your pre-departure preparations and excitement, but it is well worth it on many levels. Doing this can help you get a sense of closure, lay a good foundation for your long-distance relationships, and earn you some time upon arrival free of social obligations.

If you have ever had a close friend or relative leave home for an extended period of time, you probably remember that it was worse for you, as the person who stayed behind, than for the person actually departing. Those who leave have a great adventure to look forward to, while those who remain behind often experience a void in the fabric of their daily lives. They may also be concerned about losing their significance in the life of the person who has moved away. Taking the time to say good-bye properly may help you reassure your friends on this point, and it also gives you an opportunity to prepare them for how you plan to communicate at a distance. Perhaps you speak with your best friend on a daily basis, and he or she implicitly expects that this will continue even when you are abroad, while you know that realistically you will only be able to produce a mass e-mail once a week. This may sound trivial, but explaining what you will be going through upon arrival and sharing your thoughts on the type and frequency of communication you expect will go a long way in preventing your friends from feeling neglected—and you from feeling guilty about not living up to their expectations.

There are many possibilities for saying good-bye. Personally, I prefer to meet with my close friends individually or in small groups and spend some quality time with them, as they are the ones most likely to remain in touch. I find that large parties, catering to friends and acquaintances alike, tend to take precious pre-departure time away from the people who really matter. That being said, if you have a large group of close friends who often spend time together, such a party could work well.

Deciding Whom to Keep in Touch With

When you arrive at your destination, there are two principal temptations: (1) to postpone developing a personal life until you get work and logistics sorted out, and (2) especially if you have a large network of close friends, to want to keep in touch with absolutely everybody. Neither is very realistic. In the first case, you will find that you need friends to survive the initial period; besides, you risk damaging your relationships if you disappear for too long before trying to reconnect. In the second scenario, you will realize that you cannot treat everyone equally forever; a day has only 24 hours, your work must get done, so you will have to set priorities.

The big challenge lies really in deciding where to focus your keeping-in-touch energies. Your most rewarding relationships, those where your efforts are reciprocated, may not turn out to be the same ones at home as those when abroad. People who seemed closest to you at home can simply fade away when you move, sometimes because you mistakenly assessed the nature of the relationship, at other times because they do not have the skill or the desire to communicate at a distance. Conversely, some of your acquaintances may surprise you with their diligence at keeping in touch, and those friendships may flourish at a distance.

One way to get a sense for the relationships that have a chance of going the distance is to consider their nature. As a veteran GenXpat astutely observed, relationships are a combination of three kinds of building blocks: shared values, day-to-day activities, and common history. *Shared values* can mean a similar outlook on life due to the principles you live by or the passions you share. Both can allow you to forge a meaningful bond and reconnect even after many months or years apart. *Day-to-day activities* involve functional interactions, such as work or school, which can bring people together temporarily, but once the common forum ceases to exist the relationship often dissolves as well. *Common history* refers to having gone through some significant part of life together, which makes for a bond despite different values and day-to-day activities. The particular mix of these factors determines the viability of the relationship over distance. Though many variations are possible, four combinations stand out. In relationships with...

1. *close friends and family*, you typically share values, day-to-day activities, and a degree of common history. The values and history ensure a meaningful connection, while the activities bring you together frequently.

2. *friends*, you share values, but your day-to-day activities and history may be different, so you only get together occasionally. However, when you do meet, it feels like you were never apart—the connection is still there.

3. *family*, you have a common history, but you may not share values and day-to-day activities. The shared background allows you to get together, but you may not keep in frequent touch because the rest of your lives are so different.

4. *acquaintances*, people with whom you share day-to-day activities, you may see quite a bit of each other, more than you see your friends even, but when you stop sharing activities your connection may fade.

The relationships that involve common values and history, like those you have with close friends and family, tend to be more robust and less dependent on physical proximity than those that you have with acquaintances and other family members. The problem often lies in making the distinction between friends, with whom you share values with but see rarely, and acquaintances, with whom you spend a lot of time but share few values.

It can also be tricky to decide which family members you are close to and want to keep in touch with, and which ones you simply feel duty-bound to contact. Difficult as it may seem to make these distinctions, doing so will go a long way to helping you focus on the most rewarding relationships and make keeping in touch manageable from a time and cost perspective. It has the additional advantage of minimizing guilt.

Guilt at losing friendships is something that haunts many expatriates. You may sense that with all your new obligations, you are letting some relationships slip and you may feel badly about it. This is indeed legitimate if you go about keeping in touch on a haphazard basis, corresponding with more distant acquaintances and running out of time for those who matter. By assessing your relationships and focusing on the important ones, you have the comfort of knowing that you are doing the best possible job under the circumstances.

How Distance Impacts Relationships

Let us imagine, now, that you have successfully created a mental shortlist of your closest friends and family with whom you most want to keep in touch. As you make efforts in this direction, you discover that despite all that you have in common, some of them are not being responsive, and you begin to wonder why they are not reciprocating.

The nature of your relationship is not the only factor determining your success at connecting over distance. Another important element is finding a means of communication that works for both of you. Let me explain this with an anecdote. A regional project required me to work with a director who was based in England. I tried to kick things off by e-mail, but I never got any response. I followed up on his office phone, then on his cell. I left message after message, but he did not answer. Finally, in desperation, I sent a text message to his mobile phone. Bingo! It worked. The guy loved technology and the latest gadgets. By using text messages, as well as the website he set up, I managed to get a disproportionate amount of his time and attention. I then noticed that each person has a preferred method of communication: one of my bosses was a writer and would e-mail me even though we sat at neighboring desks; another was a talker, permanently glued to his telephone or in face-to-face meetings. The same principle holds true in the personal realm. Let us say you begin to keep in touch via e-mail and only get a 50 percent response rate. Do not immediately assume that your friends do not want to communicate with you and certainly do not get offended—yet. It could be that you are not using the right means of communication for their personality. Try several different mediums before deciding that they are not reciprocating your efforts and crossing them off your contact list.

A final factor that can impact your success at keeping in touch is the degree to which both of you feel comfortable at communicating verbally. For example, with people whom you share physical values like sports, but very little verbal communication, there may be a limit on how well you will connect at a distance. Other friends may have an "out of sight, out of mind" approach, where they genuinely like to be with you when you are physically present, but they have a hard time with the abstract nature of a long-distance relationship. In these cases, you may simply be unable to communicate at a distance, but your friendship will still be alive and well when you are face-to-face. Before you get upset or offended at their apparent lack of effort, try to consider people's personalities and see whether they could simply be poor verbal communicators.

All in all, your prime candidates for keeping in touch are your close friends and your family, though even among these there may be some who do not reciprocate your efforts until you learn how to communicate with them at a distance, and others who simply do not like distance communication at all.

Tips for Keeping in Touch

One of the main challenges of keeping in touch at a distance is maintaining the same level of intimacy that you have while meeting in person. This makes sense: most relationships involve exchanging facts and thoughts or feelings. You may not always be aware of this mix when you are interacting with someone face-to-face, but it can be striking when you begin communicating by e-mail and suddenly realize that the exchanges are somehow dry and impersonal. One reason for this is that we often transmit facts explicitly, while leaving our thoughts or feelings at least partly implicit, conveying them by gestures, facial expressions, and less-than-fully formed sentences. When we begin communicating at a distance, especially via e-mail, which requires that everything be written down and made explicit, we can end up with a lot of facts about our daily lives and lose a lot of the intangibles like thoughts and emotions.

For this reason, it may be useful to vary the means of communication you use. The typical trade-off is between expense and the degree of personal connection: e-mail is cheap but can be impersonal, while phone calls allow for some intimacy but cost decidedly more. A number of new technologies help to reconcile this paradox, such as free Internet phone services and instant messaging with audio or video functions, though their reliability depends largely on the quality of the phone or cable services at your destination.

Finally, there are visits. Having friends or family visit you can be a great way to deepen your relationship, as it allows them to get an idea of your new surroundings and better relate to your experience. Also, it can be a unique opportunity to get to know each other better than before and create memories that will cement your bond. That being said, visits are a relatively expensive and time-consuming option, because you often have to entertain nonstop. It is probably best to save them for a time when you have your new job and your relocation under control. Then there is the matter of your visits home. These can be decidedly a mixed blessing, with a crazy schedule of seeing friends, eating too much, catching up on medical visits, and shopping for things unavailable abroad. You may return to your quiet life abroad with a sense of relief, exhausted by the intensity of your supposed holiday.

As you can see, no means of keeping in touch is perfect, but using a variety of different ones can go a long way toward preserving the rich nature of your relationships.

One final thing to keep in mind as you keep in touch: do not lose sight of what others are experiencing. When you move away, the initial focus is naturally on you. Everyone wants to hear about your new job, apartment, environment, and friends. You are also naturally absorbed in the huge amount of change in your life, and it can dominate your conversations while you implicitly assume that everything at home has stayed the same. Your attitude may be reinforced by the fact that those who have stayed behind think that their lives are less interesting that yours and that you do not want to hear about them. While it is entirely normal for you to share all you are going through, do make sure you get your friends' stories as well.

BUILDING SOCIAL
NETWORKS ABROAD

7

In October 2001, Anna moved to Holland to live with her fiancé. They had met the previous year while on student exchange in Durham, England: she had been doing a research semester for her M.A. in philosophy at the University of Warsaw, while he was completing a year abroad as part of his studies in criminal law at the University of Groningen.

Anna is a vivacious girl with great social ease, fluent English, and extensive foreign experience. Thus, the idea of moving to Holland, a country where she didn't know the language or the people, seemed eminently accessible. She planned to study Dutch for a year, then to begin a degree in European law. In the meantime, she knew that she could get by with English, which is widely spoken in the Netherlands, and she didn't expect any problems making friends.

She began, as always, by letting people take their time and not trying to force things. Still, she was surprised at how long it took for the Dutch to express an interest in her as a foreigner, compared to other nationalities she had encountered. Mastering her initial loneliness, Anna resisted the temptation to sink indiscriminately into Polish circles, abiding by her personal rule of befriending only those fellow nationals with whom she would have liked to spend time with in Poland. She felt it was important to avoid falling into a pattern of trying to re-create home while living abroad. She wanted to show her Dutch acquaintances that she was genuinely interested in participating in the local way of life. Despite all her efforts, it took about nine months for Anna to experience any kind of "thaw" in her relationships with the locals.

Even then, she was often taken aback by their attitudes to friendship. In some cases, what she would have considered as appropriate behavior given a certain length of relationship turned out to be quite the opposite. As an example, she cited the situation of a Dutch lady who complained how an acquaintance of just seven months had dared to ask whether she could stay overnight, seeing that her last train home would force her to leave a party earlier than she would like. Apparently, Anna learned, it takes a much more profound friendship in Holland to justify imposing on the privacy of someone's house. In other cases, Anna was surprised at what the Dutch considered to be intimacy. She described her relationship with a Dutch girl: they had initially met at the university, then they went on to catch a movie together once in a while, occasionally going to see an art exhibit or grabbing a coffee together on the town. They would talk about school, friends, fashion, and books, but rarely

*wander into more personal matters—Anna didn't even know if her friend
had a boyfriend. So Anna was completely astonished when the girl confessed that she had never felt this close to anyone in her life! It appeared
that simply spending so much time together outside of school or work was
a sign of intimacy in Holland.*

*Three years into the game, I asked Anna to consider what had worked
well in her efforts to build a social network and what she found was still
lacking. It was, she felt, important to remain true to herself; this contributed to the development of the many pleasant and quite close
acquaintances she now has in Holland. What's missing is quite simple,
she said. She still doesn't have a close Dutch girlfriend; her best friend
there is Polish. Anna is slowly coming around to the idea that the issue is
a difference in mentality, that there can be various ways of defining friendship around the world, and that these play a role as we try to build social
networks outside our home countries.*

In the first months of your stay abroad, you may find yourself living
the proverbial French *métro-boulot-dodo*, which can be loosely translated to mean *eat-work-sleep*. Your prime focus will be on succeeding
in your new assignment, and you may be tempted to log long hours
at the office, both to prove yourself and for lack of anything else to
do. While this is a legitimate phase, it is important not to let it go
on forever. At some point, you will find that your work is under control but that you linger at the office because you do not have anyone
to head home to and no set social life or hobbies to draw you away.

During this phase, you may also find yourself relying heavily on
the friends and family you left back home, mostly because you have
not had the time to develop any relationships locally. Keep in mind,

though, that no number of e-mails or phone calls to your close ones can replace real, live people who witness your everyday joys and sorrows, even if it is on the superficial level of a new relationship.

The key to a successful life abroad is knowing how to strike a healthy balance between delivering results at work and developing a social life, as well as between your more profound distance relationships and the newer connections you forge at your destination.

Challenges Involved in Meeting People

Meeting people locally is not always easy. One limiting factor is the degree of your "foreign-ness." Paradoxically, it can be harder to get started in a country where you speak the language fluently and where you do not stand out as a foreigner. In those cases, there is no reason for the locals to single you out as an object of interest. They will continue going about their business on the assumption that, because you are fully able to function and communicate, you do not need their help to figure things out. By contrast, in a place where your physical appearance marks you as a foreigner—and as long as there is not any resentment toward foreigners in general—your local colleagues will typically be eager to share background about their country and to show you around, while the expats will be happy to see a new face in their limited circle and welcome you into the fold.

Another variable is the nature of your destination. Crawling metropolises like Tokyo, Paris, and New York City have millions of people and large expat populations, but it is easy to find yourself alone in the crowd, without access to the fairly closed social circles. In a very small town, especially those unaccustomed to foreigners, it can be hard to make inroads into the established way of life. Probably the best type of destination is a mid-sized city with a fairly large migrant young professional population. This ensures that there are entertainment venues of interest to people at your age and stage, and the somewhat transitory nature of the inhabitants means that other people are also looking to form new social ties.

Strategie for Meeting People

The following are a few strategies that can prove useful as you start spreading your social wings.

◉ *Tap into your networks.* Before leaving your home country, let your acquaintances know where you are heading and ask whether they know anyone there. Do not hesitate to take the most unlikely names and contacts: even if your grandfather's childhood buddy is out of your age range, he may have a gradnchild he can introduce you to. Your high school or university alumni associations can also be good resources. Finally, if you are part of a club or organization at home, you can ask whether it has branches or affiliates at your destination.

◉ *Get involved in scheduled, group activities.* Do you feel strongly about something, like philosophy, politics, or a social cause? Joining an organization that will help you to exercise that passion will give you the opportunity to meet people with similar values and can be a good place to start forming meaningful friendships. On a less profound level, you can try clubs centered on a particular interest, such as rowing, dancing, or Scrabble. Though such groups cannot ensure the same depth of connection, you will meet people with whom you have a pastime in common. Finally, consider signing up for some courses, like language, cooking, or fitness classes. Learning is a good way of bringing people together. Regardless of what you choose, you will likely benefit most from regular, scheduled, group activities that can discipline you to leave work at a decent hour and also overcome any timidity you may be experiencing.

○ *Cast the net wide.* The early months of your stay abroad are a kind of social brainstorming. Brainstorming involves uncritically generating lots of ideas and only stepping back to edit them after a while. Socially, you can do the same thing: at the beginning, meet as many people as you can, even if you do not expect them to be soul mates. Building a broad base of acquaintances lets you meet even more people, and you will be able to refine your selection later on. Inevitably, your first contacts are most likely going to be with your work colleagues. However, do not limit yourself. GenXpats tell of the most unlikely friendships, such as the bond they forged with a fellow shopper in their national food store or the stranger sitting next to them on the plane.

○ *Take initiative.* People tend to be attracted to those doing fun, exciting things. Rather than waiting to hear about what your colleagues or newfound acquaintances are doing and hoping they will invite you to join them, try to have your own plans and activities. Organize a house-warming party, tell your colleagues about the wine-tasting classes you signed up for, or let them know about your planned sightseeing trip. You will be surprised how many people will want to join you.

This might sound like a lot of work and, in truth, it is. Building a social network is a classic case of getting back only as much as you put in. Nothing will happen if you just sit at home and feel sorry for yourself. The more interests you have and the more initiatives you take, the greater the chance that you will meet people.

Even once you get a circle of acquaintances going, you might find that the progression of your relationships is not linear: after a rapid initial evolution, your friendship may hit a plateau that can be hard to overcome, or vice versa. The plateau can occur at different moments depending on the nationality you are dealing with. For example, Americans are famous for letting people in quite far on first acquaintance. You may be invited for after-work drinks, a game of tennis, or even dinner at someone's home very quickly. Yet this does not mean that you are admitted to the inner circle of friends, with whom one shares truly personal issues. On the other hand, Europeans can initially come across as quite standoffish: though you may spend every lunch hour with the same colleague, it may take a long time for him or her to extend a personal invitation, if ever. Europeans tend to keep work and personal lives mostly separate. However, once they invite you, this means that they consider you a personal friend.

Taking relationships to the next level, especially when dealing with adults who have well-entrenched habits, can take a long time. Think about it: if a new, foreign colleague joined your current workplace, would you have the time or the desire to include him or her into your regular social routine? As a newcomer, it is important to keep making the effort, issuing invitations, and initiating events without taking rejection personally. At the same time, you will learn to identify realistic candidates for friendship quite quickly. Married couples with young children tend to be busy and self-absorbed—quite understandably—while singles or people in life-transition may be more open to changing their routine and including you.

A final point about treating your colleagues as friends. On the one hand, doing so is certainly an easy way to meet people. You spend a lot of time with them, and if they are in a similar age range, they may be a natural place to start your social networking. On the other hand, never forget that they are your colleagues, and that sharing some of your work-related woes with them can backfire. It is also important to keep in mind that not every culture considers it appropriate to socialize at work, and even when it is acceptable to do so with your equals in the hierarchy, it may not be proper to befriend your superiors or your subordinates. All in all, while you may begin your social efforts at work, it is always best to keep going until you meet people outside of the workplace as well.

Locals or Expats?

The biggest alternative facing you as you begin to build your social life abroad is whether to try to meet locals, other expats, or both. Language and cultural factors clearly play a role in how much you can realistically integrate with the local population. If you are moving from the United States to the United Kingdom, there are no obstacles stopping you from communicating with the locals, while if you relocate from the United States to China, you must overcome the language barrier and a relatively hermetic culture to get to understand how the average person lives and thinks. Still, even in the most culturally remote places, both types of relationships can add considerable value.

• *Meeting Locals*
Meeting locals gives you an opportunity to experience a foreign culture in action and in full context. If, for example, you find the aggressive discussion style of Israelis striking within the context of your work, seeing the same kind of animation within an Israeli home, with entire families avidly arguing and then laughing in the same sentence, can help put it all into perspective. Rather than assess the behavior according to your standards, you will be able to consider it in its "natural habitat." Spending time with the locals can also help you really live life as they do—eating their foods, shopping in their stores, trying their pastimes—rather than attempting to take your habits and to make them fit into the destination country, like a square peg into a round hole. As an American in Israel, you might consider eating hummus purchased at the local market and renting a cabin "up north" for your weekends, rather than eating peanut butter and jelly purchased in an overpriced American food store and looking for a place to play baseball. By trying on the local lifestyle for size you get the most benefit out of your international experience, and that is why meeting locals is invaluable.

There is a considerable difference in getting to know the locals, however, depending on whether you are moving from a first-world country to a third-world country or the other way around. When you relocate to a developing country, it is important to realize that you will probably find yourself in the upper echelons of society. As a businessperson, it is quite likely that you will be dealing with a relatively narrow group of pretty powerful and wealthy people; people who are well-situated enough to have gotten an international education, work in a multinational company, or own a firm that is a partner for your employer. Let me make two points about this group: (a) they are most likely not representative of the average local citizen, and (b) while they may be very nice individuals, they may not have gotten into positions of power in the same transparent way that people in your country would—they may be involved in political corruption and scheming, quite incomprehensible to the average middle-class first-world expat. So be very careful about getting dazzled by the luxurious life of limousines, servants, and nightclubs that you may encounter. At the same time, keep in mind that there are also simpler local people, who may not speak much English, but who are more likely to be representative of how the average citizen lives. They, in turn, may be somewhat in awe of you. They may invite you into their homes with timidity and pride and show you off to their friends. To them, you represent the mystique of a better life. Do try to take advantage of such invitations if they are made; seeing this side of life will help put the rest of what you observe into perspective.

Meeting the locals in a first-world country is quite different and has its own set of challenges. First and foremost, people there have their own established, busy lives, and they are not likely to be particularly interested in you: there is no mystique associated with your origins. You will simply be treated as another middle-class citizen, though possibly a little lower in the rankings of potential acquaintances because you speak a different language and it is something of an extra hassle to get to know you. One GenXpat who recently had this experience summarized it nicely: "It isn't that they have anything against you, only you have to pedal twice as fast as other locals to demonstrate that it is worth their while to get to know you."

How do you get to know locals? Certainly your colleagues are a good place to start, despite the caveats I mentioned earlier. You can also join clubs or organizations that reflect local interests. For example, in Poland, golf and tennis clubs tend to attract Westerners. By contrast, hiking or sailing clubs will be dominated by Polish people. Finally, it helps to remain open to the unexpected by expressing an interest in people's lives and asking questions. Even interactions with your baker or hairdresser, for example, can offer up a wealth of opportunities.

• *Meeting Expats*

For all the advantages of meeting locals, expat friends can be worthwhile as well. First of all, longstanding expats can be good interpreters of the local culture and an invaluable resource as you learn to function in your new home, helping you with anything from medical referrals, good places to shop, or unusual tourist attractions. Especially when you are in the depths of culture shock, spending time with expats can seem like a return to "normal," where familiar cultural rules apply and people understand both your implicit and explicit communication. Do beware, however, of sinking into the expat morass. There is often a small group of malcontents who sit and complain about how terrible the destination country is, usually because they get stuck in the Regression phase of culture shock (see Chapter 4). While you may find this comforting on an occasional basis, it tends to be counterproductive and demoralizing in the long term.

○

Whenever you move abroad, it makes a lot of sense to register with your nation's embassy or consulate at destination, especially if the host country is at all politically unstable or dangerous. While you are there, ask about embassy events, clubs, or support groups that can help you meet compatriots. You can also seek out restaurants serving your national cuisine or attend events specific to your nation. For example, Canadians in many large cities get together to organize a Terry Fox Run, Poles tend to have a specific church they congregate at, and Latin Americans can be found in salsa nightclubs. If you want to meet other expats regardless of their nationality, you can visit international schools at your destination, sign up for group language classes, or even look on the Internet. Websites like *www.expatexchange.com* often have message boards on which you can connect with other expats in your host country. You can also try doing a search using keywords such as "Expats in Warsaw" or "Canadians in Warsaw" (substituting your nationality and destination, of course) and see what you come up with. In any case, with so many options to meet both locals and expats, you should have your social calendar overflowing in a very short time!

DATING ACROSS
CULTURES

Paddi, now 38, was looking for something more exciting
than the usual entry-level job in Canada. In the late '80s
the Asian economy was taking off, so he decided to enroll
in a year-long co-op program to learn the basics of doing
business in the region, and then the program set him up
with a position in the Far East. He first went to Indonesia
in 1989, working in isolated areas, and then relocated to
Kuala Lumpur in Malaysia to run a major manufacturing
facility.

In the first year of his foreign assignment, Paddi "went
native" by learning to speak fluent Indonesian, making
local friends, and dating local women. This last came
about for two reasons. First, due to the traditional Islamic
environment and his remote location, there were relatively

*few women expats present. Secondly, the Indonesian women were phys-
ically different, thus attractive. Also, his own visible foreignness and
suspected wealth earned him plenty of opportunities to date local
women, perhaps more than he would have had at home.*

*It was only when Paddi moved to Yogyakarta that he finally met
some fellow expats. The contrast was startling. While he had managed
to make good friendships with the Indonesians over two years, Paddi
connected with the Canadians in less than two weeks. It made him realize the profound role of shared history and common cultural references
in the fabric of any relationship. When it came to women, Paddi
explained, he continued dating locals for several more years; he was
enjoying the fun and exoticism of those interactions rather than looking
for a soul mate. Eventually, though, he found that he wanted the more
profound level of connection that comes from a shared background.
Religious differences were also an issue, not so much within the couple
but with respect to the outside world: often his dates couldn't tell their
families that they were seeing a Westerner because they faced a degree
of stigma within their society for doing so.*

*The opportunity to date expat women, said Paddi, came with his
move to Malaysia. Simply put, Islamic Indonesia was too traditional to
accommodate female expats, while other places, like Kuala Lumpur or
Singapore, have an abundance of talented and ambitious expat women.
Interestingly, he found that many of these ladies experience frustration
as they get overlooked by male expats, who revel in the attentions of the
locals. At the same time, expat women are unlikely to date local men,
who typically expect women to take on a more traditional role. All in
all, Paddi found that quite a bit of resentment existed among the single
female expats, and this presented a challenge when dating them. The*

other issue is that of dual expatriate careers: sooner or later one member of the expat couple must move on.

He concluded by saying that going abroad as a single worked well when he was younger and focused primarily on his career. The dating opportunities were well suited to his desire for a fun and interesting experience, but they weren't conducive to settling down. Realistically, Paddi told me, the expat lifestyle outside of North America or Europe isn't favorable for meeting your life partner, unless you're a man willing to marry a local woman. In his case, after 13 years abroad and the dissolution of yet another expat relationship, he decided it was time to head home. At this point, he would only consider another expat assignment if he could embark on it with a partner or spouse who shares his cultural background.

Challenges of Going Abroad Single

One of our particular traits as GenXpats is that we are relatively young, and many of us are single when we go abroad for professional reasons. In contrast to the traditional expat, who moves with spouse and children, we have yet to settle the personal aspect of our lives and are faced with the questions of dating abroad, maintaining a long-distance relationship with a partner who stays behind, or moving with a partner to whom we are not legally married. Each of these involves its own set of challenges, and we will look at them in this chapter and the next two.

At our age, moving as a "singleton" to a foreign country for an extended period of time does open the possibility of dating across cultures. Keep this in mind as you are making the decision to move: if you are still looking for your soul mate but are not prepared to date someone from another culture, then you are facing an important priority call between your career and your personal life. GenXpats who have decided to pursue their career without considering the cost to their private lives have often found it a high price to pay. As singles, they have no ties to any place and can fall into a pattern of moving in search of the next exciting job, city, or party. When these attractions begin to wear thin, many GenXpats return home in an attempt to settle their private lives, only to discover that their peers have long since married and started families, leaving them alone once more. If this is a concern, and you would like to marry someone with a similar background, you may want to consider postponing your departure until you are settled. However, if you are prepared to meet someone from another culture, whose values and approach to life may be very different from yours, then you are about to embark on a very thrilling, though challenging, adventure.

Dating across cultures is the most difficult international interaction of all, even more so than doing business. Why? One reason is that dating requires knowing rules interpreted primarily by implicit signals. We unconsciously absorb the nature and significance of these signals when growing up, so that as adults we can subtly communicate our interest and interpret another person's interest without exposing ourselves to explicit rejection. As a businessperson, if you are confused about the intentions of your business partner, you can often ask directly or ask mutual friends for an interpretation. The challenge in a dating situation is that you may not feel comfortable asking for the help of a third party, or the context might make it inappropriate to raise such questions. Finally, even if you are ready to ask and the person you are talking to is prepared to answer, he or she may not be able to identify and verbalize the implicit rules that are at play.

This chapter will provide you with a framework to assess the type of implicit rules and expectations likely to govern dating in your home and destination countries, to understand how this will affect you. It outlines three main types of dating environments based on some of the cultural values discussed in Chapter 5. Then it looks at the dynamics that can occur when men and women from these different environments interact: where the attraction will lie and what pitfalls can be expected.

Cultural Dating Environments

One of the important questions any culture has to resolve is the matter of the relative roles of men, women, and society in the dating or courting process. In what I call a *Liberal* environment, men and women are seen as equals, both in the eyes of the law and in terms of social expectations. In a *Mixed* environment, equality prevails from a legal perspective, but tradition and society shape gender roles, with the man as the provider and the woman as a nurturer. Finally, in a *Restrictive* environment, gender roles are imposed by the society, religious community, or legal system, typically placing men in positions of authority. These definitions of gender roles are not a matter apart from cultural values; they are directly shaped by the position a society takes on the questions of

individualism versus collectivism, low- versus high-power differential, direct versus indirect communication style, and so on.
Table 8.1 outlines how these values come together to shape each
of the dating environments. The following sections describe these
in more detail.

Table 8.1 Types and Examples of Dating Environments

CULTURAL VALUES	DATING ENVIRONMENTS		
	Liberal	**Mixed**	**Restrictive**
Personal orientation	Individual	Combination	Group
Power differential	Low	Moderate	High
Communication style	Direct	Indirect	N/A
Etiquette	Informal	Formal	N/A
Attitude toward change	Embrace	Mixed	Avoid
Location examples	U.S., Canada, Northern and Western Europe, Australia, New Zealand, Israel	Southern, Central and Eastern Europe, the secular Mideast, Latin America, Asia	Islamic theocracies, Orthodox Jewish communities

• *Liberal Environment*

In a Liberal environment, people are free to make their own decisions on most questions, including the choice of whom they
would like to date. While the input of family and friends and religious and social criteria may play a role, the choice remains
fundamentally an individual one. Furthermore, when people
choose their partners they tend to focus on personal traits, like
character, appearance, and professional achievement, rather than
considering inherited ones like power, money, or status. This is
related to the low-power differential in Liberal societies, that is,
the belief that people are fundamentally equal, and personal merit
determines a person's social status and worth rather than his or
her background.

Another area in which low-power differential transpires is in
the relationship between the genders. Liberal environments view
men and women as equal in all respects other than the purely
physical ones. Members of both genders are encouraged to get an
education, pursue professional aspirations, and be generally self-
sustaining. In terms of dating, this translates into a situation
where you have two independent individuals meeting on equal
terms. Either the man or woman can initiate contact, as there is
no prescribed "leader" or "dependent," and by the same token,
any expenses incurred while dating will be split down the middle.
As the relationship evolves into a more formal couple, the tasks
that need to get done, such as earning money, raising the children, and caring for the house, get allocated based on the skills
and interests of the two people involved. In the spirit of partner-
ship, major household decisions tend to be made jointly. In

another important aspect, if either party feels dissatisfied with the way things are going, he or she is financially able to leave.

This degree of flexibility in how relationships are set up calls for increased direct communication between men and women. It can no longer be implicitly assumed that the traditional model of the man working and the woman staying at home will hold. The division of roles is a matter of personal agreement and must be therefore openly discussed. This holds true even at the dating stage. Since men and women interact not only to court and marry but also as co-workers, classmates, and friends, there is often a need to openly clarify one's intentions.

According to traditional courting etiquette, men opened doors for ladies, and ladies interpreted a man's level of interest by the number of times he asked them to dance. In Liberal environments, the combination of belief in gender equality and preference for direct communication means that a good deal of this has been dispensed with, making dating much more informal than it used to be.

Finally, all of this reflects how people in Liberal cultures are ready to embrace change. The lack of predefined roles for men and women is in itself a big change versus the traditional, structured way of doing things, and it also makes for constantly changing forms of dating and relationships. However, people talking directly deals with the ambiguity reasonably effectively.

In summary, in a Liberal environment, people primarily get together through personal choice and approach each other as equal partners, as both are educated and financially independent. They tend to speak directly about their intentions for the relationship and their respective roles because there is no traditional, implicit standard to refer to. The interaction is informal, and couples adapt behavior to individual circumstances and needs.

• *Mixed Environment*

In a Mixed environment, individuals are free to make their choice of partner—within a pool of candidates considered to be acceptable by their parents and other members of the community. This reflects the society's combination of individual and group orientation. The individual's choice is typically based on personal characteristics, but the definition of a suitable candidate is usually based on education, wealth, ethnicity, and/or social position. This demonstrates the function of the moderate power differential in Mixed societies, that is, the fact that while people are equal in the eyes of the law, significant differences in social background do exist. As these are almost impossible to overcome by personal effort and merit, it becomes important to maintain or improve one's social position through marriage.

The relationship between genders follows a similar pattern: while men and women have the same civil rights, these societies nevertheless believe that gender predisposes people to certain activities. Though members of both genders have access to education, these cultures tend to think that men's physical and emotional make-up make them more adept at demanding labor and competitive professions like business or politics, and they believe women are better suited to raising a family or to nurturing jobs like nursing or teaching. Dating in cultures with moderate power differential reflects the behavior of the future couple—the man typically initiates contact and takes a leading role, while the woman can either accept or decline his attentions. The man will usually pay for the date, partly as a function of his higher earning power and also to indicate that he is capable and willing to provide for his future spouse. The couple usually adheres to a traditional division of roles, with the man pursuing a professional career and the wife staying at home or having a part-time job. Major household decisions tend to be made by the man, as the primary breadwinner, while the wife is limited in the degree to which she can disagree overtly due to her financial dependence on her husband.

The fact that men have more formal power in both professional and domestic situations means that women must resort to using influence if they want to impact the way things are done. I have heard this form of indirect communication nicely summarized as "being the neck that turns the man's head." Maintaining the traditional roles also allows for a lot of things to remain nonverbal. For example, men and women interact as friends and colleagues only in the context of a group. As soon as there is a question of a personal meeting, it marks the return to traditional interaction, with the invitation implicitly signaling an expression of interest on the man's part and willingness to consider on the woman's part. During the date, as she learns more about her suitor, the woman has a whole array of implicit signals at her disposal to communicate her interest or lack thereof, without actually having to put it into words.

The heavy use of indirect communication gives rise to the need for formal etiquette. Established codes of behavior allow both parties to get to know each other and communicate without having to verbalize everything, such that if the woman is not interested, the man can read her signals without losing face. Etiquette is also linked to social status and therefore power differential: knowing the rules of etiquette signifies education, wealth, and position.

Finally, it becomes clear how Mixed societies have a varied attitude to change. From an educational and economic perspective, many are evolving to allow women into universities and the workplace. However, in the social sphere, interactions between the genders remain implicit and traditional.

In summary, in a Mixed environment, people choose their spouses based on a combination of personal preference and social expectations. The man typically initiates contact and takes the lead, in anticipation of his future role as provider. There is no need to speak overtly about mutual intentions for the relationship, because the very fact of the man's invitation and the woman's acceptance or rejection makes things clear. The interaction tends to follow certain standard, implicit rules of etiquette, which are slow to change.

• Restrictive Environment

In a Restrictive environment, the individual is not free to make a personal choice of partner. Parents or elders in the group often arrange marriages based on the wealth and social positions of the respective families. These considerations are paramount in the choice of a spouse: when dealing with a society of high-power differential, wealth, and power, social status can only be acquired by marriage and birth, not by personal achievement.

The high-power differential extends to the interaction between the genders, and is in some cases legally cemented. Boys and girls grow up strictly segregated, with boys attending school and having access to professional opportunities, while girls stay at home and learn household chores. After marriage, women are strictly dependent on their husbands for financial support and, depending on the country, are not free to travel alone or interact with men who are not related to them. Women are also subject to strict rules concerning modesty of behavior and dress. While a man can physically punish or leave a wife he is not satisfied with, a woman cannot do the same because she will be publicly condemned and will have no way to support herself.

There is essentially no communication between men and women prior to marriage, and no etiquette the man should follow to court a woman, as the nuptials are a "business" transaction arranged by third parties. Change is practically nonexistent, as unusual behavior will result in severe condemnation by the rest of society.

Diagnosing the Dating Environment

Diagnosing which kind of environment you are dealing with is fairly straightforward. You can identify Restrictive cultures by the segregation of genders, full-coverage clothing of the women, and their conspicuous absence in the workplace and other public arenas populated by men. You can usually distinguish between Liberal and Mixed societies by asking whether women can live alone before marriage and whether it is common for women to continue working in nontraditional roles, such as management, after marriage. A "yes" would indicate a Liberal culture.

That being said, you need to consider the individual you are dealing with as well. Even though the environment in a place like Montreal is by and large Liberal, if you meet an Orthodox Jew, chances are he or she will be living according to Restrictive rules, and if you meet a person of Polish or Mexican background, they may be more Mixed. The key is to understand if the person you have met is playing according to the broadly applicable local rules, or whether he or she is likely to be influenced by another background or culture.

Dealing with expats is another matter altogether. Many leave home as a chance to get away from social expectations and for the opportunity to change their behavior quite significantly. Many GenXpats temporarily enjoy the liberties of being abroad, while fully planning to resume their usual roles and places in society when they head back. That is why it is crucial to see your potential partner in his or her normal social context and understand what cultural values he or she truly lives by before making a lasting commitment.

Moving across Dating Environments

Before taking a look at how people from different dating environments are likely to interact, it is useful to keep one thing in mind: the division between Liberal and Mixed or Restrictive environments tends to run along economic lines, with Liberal attitudes predominating in first-world countries and the more traditional attitudes occurring more frequently in third-world countries. While genuine romance is possible, it is important to understand that there may be hidden agendas due to economic differences. For example, it is a well-known fact that first-world businessmen get swarmed by attractive women when they go out on the town in third-world countries. These ladies can range from professional escorts to local girls hoping for anything from a few free drinks to a passport to a better life abroad. If, as a man, you are looking for a genuine relationship, it can be helpful to ask a local friend or colleague what he or she thinks of your new date. They are in a much better position to read the hidden agenda than you are. Though this applies mostly to men in the context of business travel, it also touches Liberal women when they head south to resort destinations and get a lot of attention from attractive male members of the resort staff. Many fall in love and get married only to find themselves single again once their husbands have acquired first-world passports.

Interacting with People from Restrictive Environments

The most frequent scenario is that of a single man from a Liberal or Mixed environment being sent on assignment to a Restrictive one, such as the American employee of an oil company being sent to Saudi Arabia. It is quite rare for a single woman to be delegated in such a way, since she would be bound by many of the rules that restrict local women from interacting with men in a business context, and thus she would be less able to work effectively.

The single male GenXpat in a Restrictive environment finds himself in a difficult situation. On the one hand, local customs do not allow him to approach, let alone date, a local woman. On the other, the only foreign women present are the spouses of other expats. Bottom line: it is quite likely that he will remain single for the duration of his assignment. A variant of this situation can occur with the male GenXpat being sent to an environment where there are simply few expatriate women present, and the language or cultural barrier is too significant to consider dating local women.

If, as a potential male GenXpat, you think this situation might apply to you, take the time to learn more from colleagues who have gone through the experience. If you are at a point in your life where finding a partner is important to you, it might make sense to delay your departure until you are settled.

The secondary scenario is that of a single man from a Restrictive environment being sent abroad, typically to get his education in Europe or the United States. While he may casually date foreign women, he will probably be expected to marry a girl of his own background upon his return home.

All in all, men and women from Restrictive environments are unlikely candidates for intercultural dating and marriage because of the importance their societies place on maintaining cultural homogeny. For this reason, our discussion of intercultural dating will focus on people from Liberal and Mixed backgrounds.

Mixed Men and Liberal Women

As we have seen in the description of the different dating environments, Mixed men come from a setting where they are expected to take the lead in the courting process and women are supposed to either graciously accept or decline their attentions. Liberal women, by contrast, come from an environment where they are free to be proactive and approach a man. Their mutual attraction can be explained quite simply: Mixed men appreciate the initiative of Liberal women, while Liberal women enjoy the chivalrous attentions they receive from the men.

On a dating plane, misunderstandings can abound. The most frequent misconception held by Mixed men is that a Liberal woman's independence means sexual laxity, and this can lead to one of two attitudes. Some men choose to aggressively pursue the Liberal women visiting their countries, thinking that these women will be easier to seduce than local girls. It is very important for Liberal women to remember that in Mixed societies they should *never* allow themselves to be alone with a man outside of a strictly business context, even under the pretext of a casual, friendly meeting, unless they are prepared to be intimate with him. Other men may steer clear of Liberal women, because they are turned off by the Liberal women's aggressiveness and supposed promiscuity. In this sense, if a Liberal woman is attracted to a Mixed man who is not making any evident advances, she will actually increase her chances of success by not taking the initiative and waiting patiently for him to do so.

Of course, not all the misunderstandings are on the part of the men. The most common misconception experienced by Liberal women is overestimating the level of interest and commitment of a Mixed man. He may be calling every day, sending flowers and love letters, offering to pay for dinner, and so on. These types of behaviors are all but nonexistent on the part of men in Liberal societies today, so the Liberal woman likely assumes that her suitor is exceptionally interested in her. The truth is, he is simply engaging in his usual courting routine, and he may be doing the same with other women. If, as a Liberal woman, you are interested in a lasting relationship with a Mixed man, you should keep in mind that his society often distinguishes between the women men play with and the women men marry. The first thing to verify, therefore, is whether he has a wife or fiancée at home waiting for him. If he is indeed single, then it is important to remain the type of girl he can marry, that is, to remain modest and restrained.

Finally, if you can overcome all these dating challenges and form a relationship, there will continue to be cultural differences at play. The Mixed man typically expects to be the head of the household, the principal provider and decision maker, with a spouse who takes on a more nurturing role. The Liberal woman expects to remain independent, have her own income, and participate as an equal in household decisions and obligations. The ongoing challenge in such a relationship will be establishing a balance of power and responsibility that provides validation to both partners.

Liberal Men and Mixed Women

Liberal men come from an environment where they are supposed to act as friends and equal partners in a relationship, which can be initiated by either the man or the woman. Mixed women, by contrast, come from a setting where they are accustomed to make themselves attractive so that they will be courted or pursued by men. The mutual attraction is often based on the fact that Mixed women feel validated by their chance to be an equal partner to a

Liberal man, while Liberal men are attracted to the femininity and nurturing of Mixed women.

In a dating context, the initial approach can be tricky. Liberal men are not used to reading the implicit signals of the Mixed woman, which can be designed to encourage or discourage. On the one hand, a Liberal man may hesitate to take the initiative when this is called for, and may not have the arsenal of traditional manners and courting strategies to make himself attractive to the Mixed woman. If he does not invite her to dinner, send her flowers, and escort her to and from the home, he may appear unmanly, ill-bred, or cheap. On the other hand, a Liberal man may be encouraged by the polite smile of a Mixed woman, and fail to understand the subtle distinction between a smile of invitation and one of refusal. When moving to a Mixed environment, as a Liberal man, ask your friends and colleagues about the etiquette that must be adhered to when approaching local women, and also about how far you should take your advances. It may be that in certain environments there is a distinction between the women you can sleep with and the woman you plan to marry.

Women from a Mixed society can also struggle with meeting a mate while on expatriate assignment in a Liberal society. By and large, they wait for men to take the initiative to ask them out— and they could end up waiting forever when dealing with Liberal men! Even if a Liberal man does issue an invitation, a Mixed woman may be confused about his intentions when he expects her to suggest a venue or pay half the bill. In her mind, if a man is interested, he should take care of those things. Finally, in a Mixed society, men express their interest by asking women out, and women respond by either accepting or rejecting these advances. A Mixed woman may not realize that, after the first few dates in a Liberal society, she is expected to confirm her interest by calling the man.

This mutual lack of initiative can continue to be a challenge once a relationship develops. Most importantly, the Mixed woman will likely be waiting for a marriage proposal, while the Liberal man may be quite happy leaving things on a common-law basis. She may further expect her husband to be a provider and protector, while the Liberal man will expect her to take an active role in the household by contributing her opinions on major decisions and possibly helping financially. The ongoing issue in such a relationship will be the question of both parties stepping up to expectations.

Is Intercultural Dating Worth It?

The old adage is that opposites attract, and increasing numbers of couples are successfully bridging cultural differences and finding that these allow for a richer and more varied relationship. The most important thing is to recognize that there will be differences in expectations that are not simply idiosyncratic but are much more far-reaching, and to try to learn about these differences to find ways of working with them. In the descriptions of intercultural interactions in this chapter, I have given only a hint of the principal challenges. You can continue to do some work on you own by comparing the cultural values each of you holds according to the chart and determining the impact of the difference. For example, if you come from a Liberal environment and your partner comes from a Mixed one, you are likely to be more independent (individual orientation) while she may be more attached to friends and family (group). You may like to consult your spouse on major decisions (low-power differential), while she may think it appropriate to consult her parents (high-power differential, respect for seniority). You may like to discuss issues upfront (direct communication); she may prefer to hint at things (indirect). Understanding each other's cultural context will help you communicate and grow together.

LONG-DISTANCE RELATIONSHIPS

9

Julia, a manager at the Frankfurt headquarters of Lufthansa, was facing a dilemma. While she enjoyed the strategic nature of her work and her role in the company's center of operations, she missed the entrepreneurial spirit that one sometimes finds in the smaller, subsidiary operations. Then she heard of a business development opportunity with one of the regional airlines within the Lufthansa Star Alliance—all very informal, of course—but fun to consider. The job would be based in one of Europe's mid-sized historic towns with a charming atmosphere. Julia hurried home to share the idea with Stephan, her partner of over a decade.

It was lovely to know that she would see him at the end of her workday. For more than two years, she had been in

*Zurich while he remained in Frankfurt. They had tried to find opportunities that would accommodate the progression of both their careers. Unfortunately, his profession required that he live in one of the principal European financial centers, such as Frankfurt, London, or Paris, while her role as a marketing manager within a consumer goods company took her to the cities that housed the firm's offices or plants. As a couple, Julia and Stephan had accepted this reality and decided to go with the **split-family** terms of her expatriate assignment in Zurich. Her contract provided funds for her to return to Frankfurt every weekend, and that had to be good enough.*

At this point, the full implications of Julia's new opportunity sunk in: once again, she'd have to decide how her relationship would fit with her career interest. Although the long-distance interaction between Frankfurt and Zurich had been positive overall—she was still with Stephan—it hadn't been without its toll. Jetting back and forth between the cities, Julia had found herself with two apartments but no real home. She hadn't been able to create a real social life in Zurich, as most events happened on weekends, when she was away, and people naturally were less interested in an acquaintance who couldn't be counted on to be present. She had also lost touch with many of her friends in Frankfurt, as she chose to focus her time there on being with Stephan and furnishing their new apartment. She cringed as she recalled the slight tension that had developed between her mother-in-law and her during this time. Seeing that Stephan was too busy to care for himself, his mother had undertaken to purchase some domestic items and fill some housekeeping gaps. And Stephan hadn't liked returning home to the empty apartment after work. It hadn't been an ideal state of affairs, but their bond had survived.

Over dinner, Julia broke the news of her opportunity. The discussion took a turn she hadn't anticipated. Stephan pointed out that when she had gone to Zurich, she was 30 and professional challenge was her principal concern. Four years later, they were entertaining thoughts of starting a family. Moving to a new location would mean that she couldn't consider having a child within the next few years: professional aspects would have to take precedence. Besides, if she were to begin maternity leave while abroad, it would make finding a post-natal job back in the home office quite challenging. Suddenly, the pieces of the kaleidoscope shifted—Julia realized that there was more than a job opportunity under discussion. It was a much more fundamental choice between career, relationship, and family aspirations that they had to address together.

Can We Make This Work?

Though some GenXpats are single when they set out on their expatriate assignments, as we saw in the last chapter, many are in more or less established relationships without actually being married. This last is very significant. Very few married couples would agree for one of the partners to head off on a long-term business posting abroad while the other stays behind. Yet this is quite a frequent phenomenon among couples that are dating or even living together. Why is it so? I believe that the distinction between marriage and "living together" shows up in instances like these. The commitment of marriage is, among other things, that of valuing the relationship over career considerations, with either the potential transferee refusing the expatriate assignment or the spouse agreeing to move (more on that in the next chapter). It is the unmarried couples that are far more likely to envisage having their careers and their relationships too.

The willingness to embark on a long-distance relationship (LDR) could be due to a combination of factors: that both partners are still at early stages in their careers, feel that they have yet to prove their merit, and are not in a position to present personal considerations in the choice of an assignment. They may also feel that it is too early in the relationship to know whether it is worth giving up a career opportunity for. As a result, they choose an option that seems to reconcile these conflicting needs—they accept a foreign posting and opt to remain together over a distance.

What may not be immediately apparent to these couples is the level of commitment required for the success of a LDR. LDRs require a significant investment of time and money, and very often sacrifices in time spent with friends and on personal pursuits. They actually require far *more* effort than a regular face-to-face relationship. For this reason, they are unlikely to work if the couple embarks upon it out of uncertainty, especially uncertainty that the relationship is worth giving up a career opportunity for.

Requirements for a Successful Long-Distance Relationship

Let us look at some of the factors that can contribute to a successful LDR. First of all, both partners must have a clear understanding about the degree and nature of their commitment to each other. Both must go through the exercise of asking themselves some of the following questions: Can I articulate why I love this person? If so, why am I prepared to choose a career move over my relationship? Is this an exceptional circumstance that we are both committed to correcting as soon as possible, or are we really just trying to put off making a choice between our careers and our relationship?

It may seem rather cold and calculating to detail why you love your partner. However, it can be very useful to have this in mind when your relationship comes under attack. And it will: by virtue of the sheer exoticism and attraction of the people you will meet abroad, physical separation from your partner, challenges in distance communication, fewer opportunities for shared experiences, and many more things. Thus it is helpful to be able to articulate the unique nature of your bond. Apart from sheer attraction, you can analyze it in terms of some of the same factors that make strong friendships, thinking of the values, history, and daily activities you share. Knowing what these are and how hard they are to replace will help you keep more insignificant passions at bay.

Secondly, it is vital to have a clear timeline for getting back together. For most people, an LDR can only work as a temporary situation, a brief period where career takes precedence over relationship, rather than as a lifestyle. Take the time to discuss with your partner how long he or she is willing to spend apart, keeping in mind that most expat assignments last about two years. Once the two of you reach an agreement, communicate it to your employer *before* the assignment begins. This is important, because expat assignments often get prolonged, and the employer usually feels less of a sense of urgency about finding you a job back in your home country than you and your partner do. Being upfront about where you plan to draw the line and reiterating this as time goes on will make it clear how serious you are. That being said, it may well be that your employer never does get around to sending you home. In that case, you may have to honor your commitment to your partner by quitting your job and staging your return independently.

Finally, it makes sense to agree on a trial period with your partner. Even with a clear commitment to each other and a timeline for getting back together, you may find the reality of keeping a relationship alive over a distance too much for either one of you. You might like to set a deadline vis-à-vis each other, say six months, when you plan to review how things are going: Are you both comfortable with the arrangement? Are you both getting all you would like out of the relationship? Are there any changes that need to be made, more frequent meetings, for example? You might even like to let your employer know that you have made this kind of arrangement with your partner. That way, you signal the importance of your relationship upfront, paving the way for potential contract renegotiation.

It really takes all of these—clarity on the immense value of your current relationship, a good reason why you are temporarily ready to give it up in favor of your career, and an open line of communication with both your partner and your employer—for a long-distance relationship to have a fighting chance.

Impact of Distance on Relationships

If you are currently living with your partner, then the transition to living apart, in another city, country, or time zone, can impact both of you on many levels. To begin with, there is the loss of physical intimacy. Then there is the loss of your most constant companion, the person who knows the most about you and who is present to share your daily ups and downs. Finally, there is the change in your relationship dynamic. You will no longer have access to all the details of your partner's existence firsthand. If your relationship previously had three pillars—shared values, history, and day-to-day activities—you will find that suddenly the latter one is being yanked away. Different relationships have a different mix of these three factors; if yours was heavily dependent on the things you *do* together, this could have a major impact.

Friends and colleagues who have had successful LDRs report that it is necessary for the partners to see each other once or twice a month. Longer intervals can be allowed to occur occasionally, but it would be unrealistic to expect a relationship to work if you can only see each other a handful of times a year for a few days at a time. At that point, it is likely that the benefits of meeting someone new at your destination would soon outweigh the benefit of the connection you have with the partner you have left behind.

Fairly frequent meetings are not only key to maintaining intimacy; they are necessary to defray the weight of expectations that these meetings can engender. Many times couples postpone various issues until they can see each other face-to-face. The expectations of those meetings then become tremendous: on the one hand, the couple wants to recapture the romance of the relationship, on the other, there are lots of logistics, decisions, and issues that need to be dealt with in the span of a weekend. The short time you have together is further hampered by the accumulated tiredness of an intense workweek combined with the exhaustion of travel. It can therefore be hard to get on the same wavelength and satisfy each other's expectations, and very easy to fall into petty squabbles instead. The more frequent and ordinary you can make the reunions, the better, as there will be fewer things to catch up on and less pressure to make them perfect.

For the sake of providing a complete picture, I will mention that some people actually enjoy the long-distance setup. They find the rare meetings a good way of keeping the excitement of a first date, and like the fact that they do not have to share the mundane elements of daily life. This is less likely if the couple has been living together for a period of time before the onset of the LDR; more often, the couple will have met during a trip, semester, or internship abroad and the LDR consists of joint holidays. Such an arrangement allows the couple to combine occasional romance with the benefits and space of conducting a bachelor lifestyle at home. The main challenge of these "holiday" LDRs usually occurs when the couple attempts to live together full time and make things work every day. Some make the transition beautifully, while in other cases both parties realize that they really liked having independent lives and they break up.

Communication

As we saw in the chapter on keeping in touch with friends and family, differences in communication styles or the inability to verbalize emotions can pose a problem over distance. If you consider that romantic relationships have an even greater nonverbal component and involve more intimate emotions than friendships, you can see how the problem can get compounded. For an LDR to succeed, both sides must feel comfortable expressing their feelings for each other verbally and explicitly. Another challenge of communication is what I will call *emotional a-synchronicity*. Let us imagine, as an example, that one partner—the man—has decided to go out with friends, while at the same time the woman is sitting in her foreign home, alone after an atrocious day at work, wanting to share some concerns. When she calls him, she hears the sounds of merrymaking in the background and, even though she knows that her partner is not in a position to anticipate her state of mind at a distance, she feels resentful that he is not available with his support. Differences in time zones can have a similar or worse impact: if one partner wants to make a late-evening phone call and a have a personal conversation while the other is in the midst of a morning crisis at work, chances are that they will not connect in a meaningful way. Being attuned to each other's emotional needs at a distance can be tricky. One strategy is to set aside regular times and channels for "serious" discussions, which ensure you are both in a private setting and available to talk and share. Another is to practice the art of listening: by staying quiet and receptive long enough, you will eventually create the opportunity for your partner to share what is on his or her mind. Many personal concerns take some working up to, and pauses are a natural part of that, though they can often feel uncomfortable on the phone. Learning to use the phone in an effective way is an essential skill of LDRs.

Straddling Locations

Another aspect of LDRs is that you may find yourself "straddling" two locations, without really settling down in either one. It begins when you spend most of your nonwork-related time traveling home to see your partner. This means that you never have the time to properly settle into your new apartment and purchase all the knickknacks it takes to make a home, nor do you have the time to settle into your new city, meet people, and visit its attractions. Your weekday evenings end up consumed by the chores required to maintain households in two different cities, while you dedicate your weekends to couple time at the expense of other friendships. This last is something to be very careful about.

If you consider that most LDRs have the odds stacked against them, it is particularly important to maintain your other friendships in case things do not work out with your partner. Consider what would happen if you have spent the better part of your first year on assignment jetting back and forth between home and abroad and your relationship ends. Suddenly you realize that you are alone in a new city, but you are no longer a newcomer. The acquaintances you have in your host country have gotten used to the fact that you are never around, and no longer make the social openings they did when you had just arrived. Simultaneously, you have lost touch with your friends back home, because you never made time for them. You can find yourself in a very lonely place. To prevent this, be very disciplined about keeping work within reasonable limits and making the effort to build a social life at destination, no matter how tired you are after your workday. It is also useful to ensure that your partner comes to visit you as often as you return home. This lets you discover the host country and make new friends together.

Trust

So far, we have looked at the mechanics of LDRs—commitment, communication, and handling life in two locations. Beyond that, there are certain mental or psychological requirements for an LDR to work. Probably the most significant one is the question of trust. If you do not trust your partner, then you can drive yourself crazy worrying about the temptations he or she will encounter. If you trust blindly, then you may have unpleasant surprises in store for you. What, then, are the components of a proper trusting relationship?

To begin with, you need to have confidence in yourself and your own value. If you are not entirely sure of your own merits, you may be susceptible to the constant, nagging thought that your partner may at any time find someone better, more attractive, intelligent, or wealthy than you are. The second element is confidence in your partner's ability to see and appreciate your value. If you have a subconscious suspicion that your partner is only attracted to you for superficial reasons, that could easily be superseded by someone else, or if you are concerned that your partner is not really sure of what he or she wants, and therefore why you are important to him or her, then you will likely be haunted by doubts. Only if you are fundamentally convinced of your own value and your partner's ability to recognize it, will you really feel that you are in a position to be trusting.

Of course, you cannot eliminate the possibility of your partner meeting someone else. This holds true even if you are not apart. However, if you feel confident that you both represent a consciously acknowledged value for each other, then you can trust that your partner will not be swayed by a spur-of-the-moment reaction but only by a serious feeling, and that he or she will likely discuss things with you in a forthright manner should something like this occur.

Another challenge is striking the right balance between acting as individuals and yet not growing apart. As with the question of trust, this is essential to any relationship, but distance simply puts more emphasis on the matter. Acting as individuals means keeping up or developing your own interests and circle of friends apart from the relationship. Having this kind of outlet is very important, because it allows you to grow as a person and helps ensure that you fuel your relationship with novelty and interest. It also provides a safety net to fall back on when going through difficult times with your partner. Growing apart means that, in the process of pursuing your own interests, you develop in some meaningful way that does not include your partner. Suddenly you find that you no longer share some major values, spend little time together, and really do not share very much anymore.

In a long-distance scenario, there is clearly potential for growing apart. The person who leaves is suddenly exposed to new horizons: new values, new ways of doing things, and new opportunities, and may simply cease to find understanding with the one left behind. There is no foolproof way to prevent this; the changes may be too great to bridge. Your best chance to avoid this is to have very open communication. Invite the partner who has stayed behind to visit as soon as possible, so that he or she gets a firsthand sense of what you are going through and feels part of it. Try to be frank about what you are experiencing. Let us imagine, for example, that back home you come from a middle-class environment and at your destination you are suddenly projected into high society with all the trappings: five-star restaurants, parties, limousines, beautifully dressed and powerful people. It can be tempting to get caught up in that whirlwind without sharing it with your partner back home, partly because you are scared it could make your partner feel jealous or threatened, and partly because it is too fresh even in your mind to know what to make of it. Try to talk about it and share things as they happen. The more you bottle up, the more your partner will feel excluded, the bigger the rift of understanding will be, and the tougher it will be to bridge it.

As the one who gets left behind, if you sense that your partner is sharing less about his or her life than you would like and you sense that he or she is slipping away, do resist the temptation to cling with constant phone calls and questions. Your partner is going through a big change in lifestyle and may need time to process it before sharing. Your best bet is in fact to pursue your own interests and keep developing as an individual, so that you keep pace, in your own way, with the dynamic growth your partner is going through.

Another possibility is that all your new experiences overwhelm you, and you cling to your partner at home for support. All the while, your partner at home has his or her own life and finds it difficult to deal with the sudden increase in your reliance on the relationship. You must be prepared to invest the time and effort to develop your own circle of friends and your hobbies abroad, for your own sake as well as that of the relationship.

○

Despite all your efforts, things may not work out. Out of respect for your partner, communicate any doubts you may have as early as you can. Talking about things gives you a chance to address the issue or to decide that you want to call it quits. Either way you are ahead: either you solve the issue, or you are both free to pursue the next relationship that will ultimately make you happy.

MOVING WITH YOUR PARTNER

Dor (32) and Lital (28) are now married with a two-year-old daughter, a son on the way, and three joint relocations under their belts. I spoke to each of them separately about their initial decision to go abroad together six years ago. Their stories were very consistent—probably the best testimony for the success of their relocations—but they still reflect the difference in perspective of the working partner and that of the accompanying one.

Dor told me: "We had known each other since we were teenagers, but we only began dating when Lital was in her first year at university. By then, I'd already graduated and I had my own business making corporate gift packages. She was living in Tel Aviv, and I was spending a lot of time at her place. Even so, it wasn't clear to either of us that this was 'it.'

"It was about six months into our relationship when I heard that P&G was recruiting managers for its Israeli business, which was head-quartered in Geneva. It struck me as a good opportunity to get marketing training from a world-class company, so I applied. I told Lital about it from the first; she went through the whole recruitment process with me. Despite my excitement at the idea of an international move, I knew that I had a successful business in Israel, and I made it clear to Lital that it was up to her. If she wanted to join me in Geneva, we would look at ways to accommodate her needs. If she didn't, then I would stay in Israel. There was no question in my mind that our relationship was the most important thing.

"When the time came to decide, she talked a lot with her parents. She wanted to complete a degree in psychology, but she didn't speak French. We spent a lot of time on the Internet, researching options that would allow her to complete her education in Switzerland. We also talked to other Israelis in Geneva about the paperwork she needed to move there, since P&G wasn't in a position to help.

"Once we got to Geneva, she started taking four hours of French courses per day, with the objective of passing the certification required to enter the University of Geneva the next year. Even though this kept her busy, I knew that the days were long for her in a city where she didn't know anyone, so I made a point of coming home every day at 6:00 P.M. I also felt responsible to help her find a job, since her student visa allowed her to work for up to 20 hours a week.

"Overall, there were no major issues, though I do remember that she came to see me at work after her first day at university, drowning in tears. She showed me her notes: one-third were in French, one-third in English, and one-third in Hebrew. I helped her contact people who had

been through a similar experience, to get perspective, and this reassured her somewhat. After that, it didn't take her long to adjust: in a couple of months, she was on top of the coursework, she had made friends, and she was loving the international experience."

Lital told me:

"We were dating for six months when Dor applied to P&G. The process took a long time and we were kind of left hanging. We were together when he got his answer. He said that he wanted to go because it was a good opportunity, but that there was no doubt in his mind that he would stay if I didn't want to go. This was great because I never felt that our relationship was in jeopardy. As for myself, I thought it would be an adventure for me, too...

"The biggest question was our relationship. I was only 22, we'd only been dating for a short time, and things had been on-and-off during the two months of the application process. The move put pressure on us to decide about our relationship then and there, in the same way that moving in together would, only that it involved going to a different country! Apart from that, I was concerned at leaving my family and about what I would be doing in Switzerland. I was in my first year at university, so it was important for me to finish my studies, but I didn't speak French and it wasn't clear that I could learn it well enough to do a degree in psychology. Finally, I decided to try. I was lucky to have the support of my parents and to know that I had the means to come home if things didn't work out.

"Preparation was critical. We spent a lot of time trying to figure out on what basis I could stay in Switzerland, given that we weren't married. The basic option was the renewable three-month tourist visa, but that would mean going back and forth to Israel. We considered getting married to facilitate the paperwork, as spouses are automatically granted a residence *permit, but we decided against it: we felt it was too early and that it was important to do it for the right reasons. Finally, I learned that I could have a student visa both while taking intensive French courses and while studying. It also proved useful to make sure I got all the right transcripts for my university application translated and notarized before we left.*

"The first few months were the toughest. Dor had a framework throughout his move: he had his job at P&G. I had no framework: I had been a student in Israel, but the move created a year of forced, unplanned 'time out' for me. This meant that I had to find my own inner justification for being in Geneva, and it wasn't always clear. I didn't know anyone, I was overwhelmed by the foreign language, and it wasn't obvious that I would master it well enough to be able to study. I remember one day, when we were still in our temporary accommodation, I was watching TV in French and doing housework. I felt like I was in a movie. 'What the hell am I doing here, ironing some guy's shirts? Is this my future?'

"To be fair, Dor was awesome. He always made a point of being home early and of including me in his life—telling me about his work and introducing me to his colleagues—while I was still working to create mine. It wasn't always easy to meet people who already seemed to have a clear direction, while I was still in the process of self-definition. Dor would talk to me for hours, helping me put things in perspective, reminding me what I had come to achieve. I promised myself to stick it out for a year.

"The big breakthrough came when I started university. At first it was tough, but after that things sorted themselves out. The program was

incredible, much more personalized than in Israel, and I loved it. I made my own friends. That's when I started feeling good about things.

"Overall, the experience was incredibly rewarding. I learned a new language, experienced a top-notch psychology program, made new and meaningful friendships, and also learned how to snowboard! Most importantly, though, our relationship was made stronger. When it's just the two of you in a foreign land, and there aren't any family or friends to turn to, you have to sort things out between yourselves, right away. That kind of communication cemented our bond, and took our relationship to another level."

Partner versus Spouse

Much has been written about the classic scenario of the senior executive going abroad with his wife and children. If you are a GenXpat moving abroad with your partner, you may certainly find some of this literature relevant, including Robin Pascoe's book, *Culture Shock! Successful Living Abroad: A Wife's Guide.* That being said, the case of the GenXpat is again distinctive for a number of reasons.

Typically, the GenXpat is not yet married, but simply living with his or her partner. Despite the increasingly frequent view that a marriage act is a dispensable piece of paper, when dealing with immigration authorities, papers do count. Jennifer White, Global Client Services Director at Primacy Relocation, reports that she has seen couples actually get married to fulfill the requirements of the host country. In the case of married couples that relocate, the accompanying spouse usually has a right to a residence permit and is covered by the working spouse's benefits. However, in the case of unmarried couples, countries rarely legally recognize the accompanying partner and, as such, he or she must file an independent application for a residence visa, which is typically only granted if the partner is sponsored by a potential employer or an academic institution. If the country does not grant the residence visa to the accompanying partner, then he or she can only enter the destination country on three- or six-month tourist visas, and will be denied things typically open to residents only, such as the right to open a bank account or be a co-signatory on the partner's account, rent an apartment, and buy a car (the details vary based on the destination). Even if the accompanying partner does obtain a residence permit, this is not the end of the troubles: he or she will have to independently purchase costly international health insurance and will not benefit from the support that companies offer to accompanying spouses, such as language lessons or career support. Finally, a residence permit is not equal to a work permit: most countries only grant these on the express request of the potential employer, and few employers are willing to go through the extra paperwork, costs, and hassle of making such a request.

The second difference of GenXpats is that they are younger than the classic executive expatriate couple, in which the husband works and the wife takes care of school-age children. More often than not, GenXpats and their partners are both active professionally and still childless. Many envisage dual-career futures for themselves, even if they do plan to have a family. If one partner wants to move abroad, the question of the other partner's career becomes critical and does not come with easy answers.

When I was faced with the option of relocating to Tel Aviv, to help open the local Procter & Gamble subsidiary, the opportunity seemed too good to miss. The only drawback was the question of my relationship: would my Swiss boyfriend, who held a back-office position in a Swiss bank, be able to join me? I made a strong sales pitch to him in favor of the move, listing seemingly endless job opportunities—the Swiss consulate in Tel Aviv, Swiss banks with operations in Tel Aviv and Israeli banks with operations in Switzerland, multinational companies that do business in English...not to mention that he could spend time at the beach during breaks in his job-hunt.

Once we got to Israel, things suddenly looked very different. Local companies pretty much refused to hire someone who had no work permit and did not speak Hebrew. My boyfriend had little chance of getting a work permit because he does not have a Jewish background, and priority was being given to the large influx of new Jewish immigrants. Also, he was understandably unenthusiastic about learning Hebrew because the language is so different from French and English, and because it has little chance of re-application outside of Israel. As the weeks of job-hunting turned into months, my boyfriend finally decided to give up looking for paid work and chose to volunteer. He ended up working at an animal shelter, cleaning cages and caring for the animals. Though he liked the work, this was not a solution that could have lasted for more than the eight months we spent in Israel.

As this example shows, finding a job abroad is very difficult for work permit and language reasons. The accompanying partner will likely remain unemployed for the duration of the expatriation, resulting in a career interruption and a gap in his or her resumé. Without a job or a family to raise, the question becomes how to occupy his or her time abroad.

Challenges Faced by the Relocating Couple

Thus, if you are a GenXpat thinking of moving with your career-oriented partner, you may actually be facing some tougher challenges than the traditional executive. It may be helpful for you to pause and consider the impact of the proposed move on your partner. Understanding his or her context fully can help you decide together whether the move is right for the both of you. The following list highlights some key things that your partner may have to face or experience as a result of the move. He—I will use "he" for simplicity—will have to

1. *Quit his current occupation for you.* Regardless of whether your partner is currently studying or working, he must give up what he has chosen to do for your sake. It may make financial sense to do so, in that your combined earnings will still be better if you move, or it may make career sense, in that you have the more promising career opportunity, but nevertheless the fact remains that you will take priority over your partner. This can impact his self-esteem, unless you talk about it upfront and dis-

cuss how you can ensure that his needs can also be met. How does your partner really feel about such a situation? What can you do to make up for it?

2. *Job hunt with losing chances.* If you consider that the regular process of job applications can be difficult due to the inevitable rejections, think what it must be like if the chances are set against the seeker, due to work permit and language issues. The whole process can be extremely discouraging for your partner, especially if he has high qualifications, motivation, and ambition, yet cannot even get in the door because he is a foreigner.

3. *Depend on you financially.* Chances are that as an unmarried couple you each had separate pay checks, bank accounts, and contributed equal amounts of money to expenses, such as rent, groceries, and vacations. When your partner gives up his job, he also gives up his income. He will have to ask you for money. What is your attitude about this? How will you handle it so that he does not feel as if he has to justify himself for every item he buys? Again, it is important to discuss this upfront, so that he does not lose his sense of self-worth because he is not contributing financially.

4. *Become Ms. X's partner or simply Mr. Unemployed.* Once we begin our professional careers, a large part of our identity tends to come from our jobs. When we meet people for the first time—and we meet many when we move abroad—one of the more frequent questions is, "What do you do?" I know from my own experience that "I work for P&G" got me more points than "I am working on a book." The accompanying partner or spouse also has the possibility of becoming known by association with the working spouse or the working spouse's job: "Oh, that's the new manager's boyfriend." If your partner had his own career before moving with you, such a transition can be very difficult to deal with.

5. *Lose access to his social support networks and hobbies.* Dealing with change can be much easier when you have your family and friends nearby to support you, or if you have access to your usual hobbies and recreational activities. When your partner moves with you, he is not only going through a major reformulation of his identity, but his usual methods of diffusing stress are not readily available.

6. *Deal with too much time on his hands, leading to loneliness and boredom.* Your partner can only send out so many resumés in a day. After finishing his work, he would normally meet with friends or pursue his hobbies—only he has no friends yet and he does not know where or how to practice his hobbies. You are never around because you are too busy with your professional transition, so all of a sudden your partner finds himself alone all the time, bored, and lonely.

Overall, the relocation experience and the transition from having a career to a support role in the couple can be a serious hit to your partner's confidence. On occasion, it can even be a cause for depression, and it can certainly have a major impact on your relationship.

While your partner will bear many challenges, some of the strain may also fall on you. You may feel responsible for the difficult times you are putting your partner through, pressure to make things work for both of you, and even guilt for spending too much time at the office while your partner waits at home, or if things are not working out as planned for him.

Tips for Managing the Issues

Overall, for the relocation to be successful for you as a couple, your partner must buy into the move for its own sake. If your partner understands the risks and possibilities of the move, and sees a way to make it fit with his personal objectives, then he will take the responsibility on his own shoulders. If, however, your partner decides to move only to be with you, you will inevitably be saddled with the blame if anything does not work out.

To make sure that your partner can make his own informed decision, it is important that you paint a realistic picture of the relocation and deliberately tackle the challenges listed here. The most important point to drive home is that if your partner does not speak the language of the destination country, he probably will not be able to get a job locally. This does not mean he should not plan to job hunt, but that he should assess his interest in relocating on the premise that it is not likely he will be working in his profession. For perspective, the following are some of the routes accompanying partners have actually taken:

○ *Learning the destination country's language.* Some languages might be worth learning in the context of your partner's career. If you are relocating to a country where the native language is English, Spanish, French, German, or Japanese—the most commonly used languages in international business—then it might make sense to devote a year to intensive language courses. In most cases, this should be enough to become functional in the language, that is, to be able to work or study in the country.

○ *Earning an advanced degree.* If your partner already speaks the language of the destination country, if he is willing to invest a year to learn it, or if the destination has a relevant program taught in his native language or a language he speaks well, your partner may consider pursuing an advanced degree in his field. This can also act as a stepping stone to getting a work permit and a job at destination, though there are never any guarantees.

○ *Teaching languages.* If your partner is a native speaker of one of the more commonly taught languages, then he may be able to get a job as a language teacher, and this is one of the professions where employers are used to filing work permit applications for foreigners.

○ *Volunteering.* If your partner is comfortable with the concept of volunteer work, he could get involved in one of the many local and expatriate organizations.

○ *Starting a family.* If you have been considering starting a family, this may be a good time to do so, since your partner will be at home full-time. However, it is important to do your homework before making such a major decision. If you are not married and are planning to have children while abroad, you may want to find out how this impacts their legal status in terms of citizenship and custody. You also need to consider other things such as the medical facilities at destination, health insurance coverage, and availability of your family to help out with things.

This is by no means an exhaustive list, but it covers some of the more classic scenarios. Feel free to brainstorm additional ideas, as long as they do not involve getting the ever-elusive work permit. Once you have all the options laid out on the table, your partner needs to honestly assess whether any of them works for him.

If you value your relationship, I cannot overstate the importance of presenting your partner with a genuine alternative, that is, while you would like him to seriously investigate the possibility of moving with you, you are prepared to remain where you are and give up your professional opportunity if he does not feel comfortable with the relocation. As we have seen, the relocation entails a tremendous sacrifice on your partner's side: career, independence, family, and friends. Only by having a strong personal interest in the relocation and a sense that he can achieve his objectives as well as yours, can your partner have the motivation necessary to deal with these challenges. Otherwise, in all likelihood, he will give up and go home or harbor increasing resentment toward you, thereby destroying your relationship.

○

One final thing to consider as you discuss relocation: your long-term view of life as a couple and the relative priority of your respective careers. Are you currently putting priority on the working partner's career with the intention of swapping after two years? Or are you consciously deciding that the working partner has the more promising career and will be the driving force behind future relocations, while the accompanying partner will pursue a more flexible type of work? Because relocation is rarely a one-time thing, you both need to consider this seriously. Once the working spouse agrees to relocate for the first time, there are no guarantees that he or she will be returning home after two years. The next opportunity may well be in yet another country, so it is important for you as a couple to know where you stand on that possibility. There have been countless cases of accompanying spouses agreeing to a two-year relocation on an exceptional basis only to find that they keep getting moved around for a decade.

REVERSE
CULTURE SHOCK

By definition, it would appear challenging to find a GenXpat who is a veteran of several moves. Yet Noam, shutting the door of his Tel Aviv apartment for the last time, felt just like that: battle-worn, gearing up for Round 3.

As the cab whisked him away to the airport, his mind surveyed the events of the past five years. He'd joined a fast-moving consumer goods company in Lausanne at 26, a newlywed, fresh-faced university grad. He'd been given a challenging financial analysis job, a good income, and a beautiful, peaceful country as his playground. What an opportunity that had been to shape his life according to his wildest fancies!

Fast-forward two years: with a promotion and a divorce under his belt, he was returning home to Israel to open the new subsidiary. He was looking forward to picking up the pieces of his personal life in a familiar environment and catching up with old friends, partying, and enjoying the single life.

And then…what had happened exactly? It had begun as a growing sense of irritation with the constant pushing and shoving he experienced in Israel, not only literally, when people were in a group, but also metaphorically, as a way of being. How different it was from the cool detachment of the Swiss! The irritation was compounded by the interminable political discussions among his friends—had he really been that way as well? It wasn't that he had stopped caring about his country, but he now knew what it meant to be able to get on with one's life, without having to get worked up about every empty political declaration. He had changed.

Yes, there definitely had been a sense of detachment, even from his friends. One discussion in particular stood out in his mind. A friend—who had never met a German or been to Germany in his life—had started on the usual tirade of "shame on them…they deliberately closed their eyes to the atrocities that had been going on…" Noam found he could no longer simply nod in agreement: his immediate manager, a German lady in her thirties, was a good woman. Hell, the regional president, who was one of his mentors and a man for whom he had tremendous respect, was a German in his sixties. Though young at the time, this man remembered World War II. Noam found that he could no longer join his friend in his stance against anything German as a method of remembering the Holocaust. He knew things were not that simple.

Then there were his parents. In their eyes, their son had come home, and they were impatient to welcome him back into the tight-knit fabric

of Israeli family life: Friday night dinners, holidays, and the ever-pre-
sent pressure to find a "nice" girl, get married, and have kids. What they
hadn't counted on, and what he himself hadn't realized at the time, was
how much he had grown up in the two years of his time abroad. His
time had been fully his own to do as he pleased; he had been account-
able to no one. He could no longer return to his former role of a dutiful
son. He began to set limits around his family life and learned to rede-
fine his relationship with them as one among adults.

All in all, his return to Israel hadn't been a walk in the park. The peo-
ple he now had the most in common with were other Israeli repatriates. It
didn't matter where they had been; they had all gone through the same
process of adapting to a new place, losing their support networks, and the
feeling of being strangers in their homeland upon returning. They spoke a
common language. They understood.

So it was with mixed feelings that he was heading off for a new assign-
ment in London. On the one hand, he was sorry to leave the people and land
that he loves. On the other, he knew that his sister-in-law was right: some
part of him doesn't belong in Israel. That part is the GenXpat, which thrives
in the world of young, mobile professionals, diverse and exciting due to the
eclectic mix of backgrounds and perspectives.

Returning Home: The Hidden Challenge

The first six months of your expatriate assignment are typically the
"moment of truth" in terms of your stay abroad. That is when you
are confronted with the conflicting demands of work and getting set
up in a new place, when you experience the worst of your culture

shock, and as you struggle to sort out your personal life on both the social and romantic level. Once you make it through those few months, life surprisingly becomes more cohesive and easier. You discover that you know how to satisfy your basic needs, that there are things you like about your new location, and that you can manage the things you do not. You make the transition from survival mode to actually enjoying your life at destination.

Before you know it, your two-year assignment is almost up and it is time to start thinking about returning home...or moving on to your next expatriate position. Perhaps not as obviously, this is the second "moment of truth" in the relocation process, both professionally and personally, and we will look at each of these aspects in turn.

The Professional Aspect

Throughout this book, we have looked at the professional side of the expatriate experience only to the extent that it influences your personal life abroad. For the most part, the question of how to manage a business in a foreign country is quite separate from the question of how to manage your downtime. One crucial moment of overlap occurs when you decide that you want to come home. Though this decision may be driven by personal factors, its implementation begins in the workplace, by lobbying for a position in your home country.

Securing your next job with your employer can be quite a challenge. If you simply want to move up in the ranks at your present location, this is fairly straightforward because you naturally hear about job openings and are in daily contact with the managers making employment decisions. However, when you are looking for jobs at your home office from abroad, it can be more challenging and require greater personal initiative on your part. There are two main pitfalls to watch out for as you embark on this process.

First, there is the "out of sight, out of mind" phenomenon. Once you leave your home office, you cease being visible. When there is a job opening at the next level, the boss' instinct is to look at the managers available on site for promotion, people whose performance he or she has been seeing on a daily basis and who have been lobbying for the position. He or she may simply forget to consider you. This makes it very important to keep in touch with your mentors, bosses, and former colleagues from your home office. Otherwise you risk getting "forgotten abroad" and you may find that you need to leave your employer and look for other opportunities to return home.

The second pitfall is subtler. It can happen that your employer does remember you and welcomes you back at the home office, but puts you in a position that does not fully reflect the learning experience you had abroad. This can be a function of several things. Headquarters and home offices tend to be more structured and procedural than satellite ones. Even if you hold the same job title as you had abroad, you might find that you suddenly need to refer everything to your boss, losing much of the independence you had when you were abroad. This might leave you feeling stifled and frustrated upon your return. Or you could be put in a job that simply does not reflect the international market and management knowledge you acquired abroad, both in scope and compensation. Either scenario could have you on the job market within a few months of coming home.

In summary, you almost need to think of your change of assignment as an internal job hunt. Though ideally your company should have systems in place to manage the transition, realistically you will need to get involved. You can improve your chances by starting early—about six months ahead of the time you would actually like to move. At that stage, you would do well to remind your current manager that he or she should start leveraging his network to find you your next position within the company. You should also revive your connections with the home office, both with your colleagues—to get the current gossip—and with your mentors, to be at the top of their minds when a position becomes available. When you talk to the decision-makers about the matter of your next position, bring up the issue of how to make the most of your international experience and how to ensure you stay challenged professionally. Securing the professional side of things will go a long way to help the personal side of your re-entry. There is nothing worse than to find yourself unemployed as you are in the throes of reverse culture shock, upon your return home.

The Personal Aspect

The return home is also a personal challenge. If you settled down happily at destination, you probably found it an exhilarating ride.

You mastered a new city, discovered new tastes, sights, and sounds, and made your place among them. The thought of returning home might seem so...well, ordinary by comparison. At the same time, you will probably be looking forward to it, if only because of the chance of reviving your friendships, revisiting favorite places, and resuming activities you gave up because of the move. In a sense, there is an expectation of returning to the familiar and picking up where you left off.

In reality, things may not be that simple. It is likely that your horizons broadened significantly when you were abroad, even though you may not realize it. For example, when Caroline left Montreal to teach English at the University of Heredia, in Costa Rica, she was taken aback by the personal nature of social interaction. Over time, however, she learned to accept and enjoy the degree of mutual involvement people had in each other's lives, the impromptu visits of friends, and parties with lots of drinking and dancing. When she came home, she thought that she could continue meeting with her Canadian friends as she always had: over beer at a pub. Yet when she tried it, it just was not as satisfying anymore. It seemed frightfully staid compared to the liveliness of things abroad. This was a painful discovery to make; it meant that the friends and rituals that made up the home she had expected to find did not exist anymore. Or, rather, they existed, but her perception of them had changed.

This is known as *reverse culture shock*. If "normal" culture shock occurred upon departure, when Caroline realized that it was possible for people to show up at her door unannounced or start dancing at a moment's notice, she ultimately grew to appreciate these facts and her value system changed accordingly. This kind of warmth became desirable. Upon her return to Montreal, the Canadian way of doing things came as a shock to her. Reverse culture shock is particularly insidious because it comes at a time when we believe life is finally going to go back to normal—and we discover that there is actually no going back.

The unpleasantness of being a stranger in your own home in terms of values can be aggravated by a number of other factors. To begin with, there is the return to the ordinary. As an expat, you often get to circulate in more refined social circles than you would at home, primarily because you interact with people who have the money and education to speak a foreign language, but also because of your lucrative expat package (if you have one). Besides, you get more attention as a foreigner, especially in countries where you stand out physically from the locals. Upon your return, you become an ordinary citizen. If your initial culture shock challenged your assumptions about how the world works, including proper ways of thinking and doing things, then reverse culture shock challenges your assumptions about yourself. It opens up questions like: Who am I? How do I fit in? You may have to re-examine who you are when stripped of the glamorous trimmings of being an expat. You may also have to consider how to reconcile the values and ideas you adopted while abroad with the way things are done at home.

On a social plane, after the initial joy of catching up with your friends, life simply goes on. You may find that people do not have as much time for you as they used to. This is normal. If you think about it, your departure created a gap in their lives, which they had to fill somehow. Your return finds them busy with their own lives, and there may not be a place for you immediately. Alternately, your friends may expect that you come back and fit right where you were before you left. This is also tricky, as you will have changed during your time abroad and may not be ready to resume your old role and attitudes.

When you do get together with your friends, you might find the meetings disappointing. People will typically listen to your story for a few minutes, skim through your pictures, then move on to the trials and tribulations of their daily lives. Few, if any, will be able to discuss the socioeconomic situation of your destination country or the emotional and personal growth you experienced during your time as an expat. If you insist on sticking to the topic, they might perceive you as trying to show off; if you simply cease speaking about your travels, you may get the sense that one of the more transforming times of your life has just been obliterated as insignificant. You can end up feeling alone in the worst possible way: alone among people who used to be your friends.

Dealing with Reverse Culture Shock

Personally, I find that nothing is worse than the unexpected. The higher your expectations were regarding your homecoming, the bigger the potential disappointment. If you were not happy abroad and were anxiously awaiting your return home, you may be in for a particularly tough time. "But," you will ask, "how can I prepare for the results of changes in myself, which I am not even aware have occurred?" As always, it can be helpful to talk to people who have been through the experience. Seek out people who have been repatriated and listen to their stories of reverse culture shock, and ask them about their coping strategies.

It is important not to expect to find everything just as it was when you left. It can be helpful to think of your return as a move to an entirely different place, as if you were not coming home but moving to a third location entirely. Be prepared to do things differently. Consider living in a different part of town. Think of it as a chance to redesign your life rather than fall into your old routines. How can this be helpful? If you try to reproduce your life as it was before you left, you will inevitably find changes, often unpleasant ones: your favorite neighborhood shop may have closed, your friends may not all be waiting for you, things you formerly found exotic may be dull. In a sense, you will be a victim of the changes; they will be happening to you. If, on the other hand, you proactively decide to do things differently, you will be leading the change. You will be creating new opportunities for yourself that will outweigh the losses, and you will be able to fit in parts of your former lifestyle, while leaving yourself the space to include new elements that reflect the ways you have changed.

Socially, you might find it useful to seek out other people who have been abroad, who have visited the country you were sent to, or who are natives thereof. They will be in a better position to acknowledge what you have been through than some of your friends who have never left home. Seek out restaurants that serve the cuisine of your host country or stores that sell its products. Find out if there is a community center for people of that nationality and look up events that you might like to attend. Volunteer at that country's embassy or even at your local international school to act as a guide for expats who come to your country. You might discover a whole immigrant community in your hometown that you were not aware of before, and that can add richness to your life upon your return.

More than anything else, it is important to realize that reverse culture shock can be as potent as the regular kind, that it can follow the same phases and take as much time to overcome: three months, six months, or even a year, depending on how long you were away. Do not expect to be 100 percent up to speed on the day you return just because you are returning "home." You will be facing exactly the same issues as when you were leaving: house hunting, paperwork, adjustment to a new job, building social networks, adjusting to a new environment with your partner. Give yourself time to cope emotionally with all the changes…and then start thinking about your next foreign assignment!

CONCLUSION

As GenXpats, we head abroad at a time in our lives—between the ages of 24 and 39—that is universally one of self-definition. One of the interesting themes that transpired through the stories I heard was that of shifting priorities. By and large, GenXpats are among the more ambitious and driven graduates, eager to pursue the best career opportunity that presents itself regardless of the location or of the personal implications. Your desire for challenge and adventure overrides other considerations, at least initially. Over the course of several moves, as you experience a variety of lifestyles and relationships, you develop a better sense of what is really important to your happiness and what factors can override the next exotic location or sexy job opportunity.

In Chapter 1, Zoha told us how, initially, her decision was driven by the need for change and adventure, while the specifics of her destination did not matter as much. Over time, she learned to consider certain personal and environmental factors, such as her partner's career and the cultural values at her destination, over the simple desire to move. When Paddi (Chapter 8) spoke to me about dating across cultures, he explained how, in his early twenties, having a successful career in a foreign location and dating exotic women was just what he needed. With time, he realized that he wanted more depth in his relationships and that he valued the connection that came with dating people of a similar cultural background, which ultimately contributed to his decision to return home. In Julia's case (Chapter 9), she realized that while another expatriate assignment would make for an exciting career opportunity, it would take her away from Stephan and stand in the way of starting a family. For each of these GenXpats, the foreign experience has led to a greater awareness of themselves and their priorities.

Expatriation also encourages an evolution of your outlook on the surrounding world. As one of my interviewees put it, while living abroad you learn that every culture, every person, every place has its own way of functioning, its "inner logic." Understanding this makes you paradoxically both more tolerant and more selective. You become more tolerant as you learn to accept that there are many ways to live a life and perceive the world, each of which can be satisfactory in its own way. At the same time, you become more selective as you witness all the world has to offer, and realize that you have the liberty of deciding which solutions you prefer and work best for you.

In this sense, the GenXpat experience can be a great catalyst for growth. Living in a foreign environment challenges your view of yourself and the world, encourages you to reconsider your position, and ultimately allows you to come through with a more consciously and consistently held set of values and beliefs.

The purpose of this book was to systematically discuss the areas in which you are likely to have to make a decision or take a stance during your expatriation, be it the negotiation of your contract, the confrontation with another culture, or the question of how to handle your personal life. I hope it has provided you with a useful framework to structure your thinking, to ask the right questions, and to find your own answers, and that it will help you have an enriching expatriate experience.

APPENDIX A
The Look-See Trip

The Look-See Trip is an essential tool as you prepare to negotiate the fine print of your contract. Some employers only offer it once you have accepted a foreign posting. However, the more exotic or unfamiliar the destination, the more sense it makes to check it out before committing. If your employer does not feel comfortable financing your visit ahead of time, then perhaps you can reach an agreement whereby your costs are refunded if you agree to the assignment. Another objection can relate to confidentiality: your employer may prefer not to send you over until you are confirmed as the candidate for the new assignment. In such a case, you can consider meeting with an external relocation or real estate agent only, without visiting the offices at destination. Regardless, I cannot overstate the importance of seeing what you are getting into ahead of time, even if it means going at your own expense and on your own time. If you are considering moving with your partner, it is important to go together, as this will allow your partner to explore career or occupation options.

Making a success of your Look-See Trip takes a bit of preparation. Ideally, you should ask your HR manager to put you in touch with at least one local employee and one expat with a similar background to yours, who has been at the destination country for at least six months. You should aim for contacts of the same sex and a similar age and family situation as you are. Contact them before your trip and try to set up informal meetings over lunch or dinner to discuss what is on your mind. You might even like to send them a list of questions in advance, especially a request for suggestions regarding good areas to live in given your family situation and social/recreational interests, as this will be useful when you brief your real estate agent on your housing requirements.

When speaking with the expat, you get the outsider's perspective on living at your destination, the advantages and disadvantages of the location when compared to your home country, things that you might like to bring, and things you are likely to miss. Ask about social life and cultural aspects: learn what expats do after work. Do not hesitate to seek information on what could be touchy subjects. If you are planning to move as a single, find out about the dating scene. If you are a woman from a liberal environment moving to a more traditional environment, try to understand what it can mean in terms of your usual activities; for example, can you walk home alone after dark? If your racial features are likely to set you apart from the general population at your destination, you might like to learn about the possible consequences. I mean this in the broadest sense: a blonde female colleague of mine on assignment in Egypt told me she was regularly groped by male passersby, even when walking with her husband and her baby in a stroller! In a similar vein, a black Kenyan colleague who moved to Poland shortly after the fall of the Iron Curtain told me that she often got pointed at, simply because few people in the homogeneous white population had ever seen a black person. One thing to keep in mind as you ask questions is to be specific but open-ended. For example, you might ask, "How does the political situation in Israel affect your lifestyle?" rather than, "Aren't you terrified of all the bombs?" In this way you open the door to a more comprehensive, unbiased answer.

Unless the local you are interviewing has traveled, it is unlikely that he or she will be able to give you comparative answers. Your best bet is to ask about his or her lifestyle: what kinds of things he or she does after work or on weekends. Also, do inquire—diplomatically—about things like the importance of religion, tradition, role of men and women, and so on. This will help you get an idea of cultural differences, as described in Chapter 1 (in the section "External Circumstances to Consider") and in Chapter 5.

If you are organizing your trip independently from your employer, a good place to look for contacts would be your nation's embassy or consulate at destination. You can also try searching the web for newcomer's groups in the host country or posting a question on expat websites like *www.expatexchange.com.*

Apart from interviews with locals and expats, the other vital part of your Look-See Trip is the meeting with your relocation consultant or your real estate agent. Ideally, you should be able to brief him or her on the areas you wouldd like to live in, based on the input you got from your local and expat interviewees. It is important to make your own suggestions as well to ensure that you get a range of options, as the real estate agent works on commission and may focus on the more expensive areas unless specifically told otherwise. Ask the relocation consultant about permit formalities, safety and health issues including preventative measures like vaccines, the health care system at destination and the initial referral to a physician or dentist, and career advice for your partner, as well as lifestyle and entertainment matters—availability of fitness facilities, libraries, community clubs, and the like. The real estate agent can help you with more technical things like the best strategies for commuting to work, availability of parking, and the proximity of stores and facilities. A good strategy when preparing your questions is to consider what you do over the course of a normal month in your home country—these will be all the things you will want to ask about during your Look-See Trip. Arm yourself with a notebook, and question away. When you wrap up, you might find it helpful to close with an open-ended question like "Is there anything else I should know or ask about?" Say it with a smile and a pause: you may be surprised and grateful at what is offered.

Everything you learn will help you set the right expectations, bring proper equipment, and, most importantly, negotiate your contract. For example, if you find that the area you plan to live in is central, you may decide to ask for a higher housing budget but forgo a car. If you learn that your regular 10k run will be impossible because your destination is not appropriate for running outside, you can try to ask for a gym membership with your package. The bottom line: the more you learn about how your needs will or will not be met at destination, the better you will be able to tailor the package to your needs.

APPENDIX B
Cost-of-Living Calculator

Table B.1 Example of Using the Cost-of-Living Calculator

	MONTREAL (CAD - Canadian Dollars)	GENEVA (CHF - Swiss Francs)
Gross Salary	80,000	140,952
Tax Rate (national)	20.5%	0.0%
Tax Rate (regional)	20.0%	22.3%
Unemployment Insurance	2.0%	1.5%
Old Age Pension Contribution	5.0%	5.1%
Other Deductions	0.0%	3.2%
Net Salary	42,056	95.847
Monthly Lodging Expenses	800	1,200
Annualized Lodging Expenses	9,600	14,400
Monthly Living Expenses Home	1,300	-
in CHF (1 CAD = 0.95 CHF)	-	1,235
Cost of Living Factor	-	2.1
Est. Monthly Expenses Living Abroad	-	2,594
Annualized Living Expenses	15,600	31,122
Total Annualized Expenses	25,200	45,522
Net in Pocket	16,856	50,325
in CAD (1 CHF = 1.05 CAD)	16,856	52,842

Appendix B gives you a basic tool to compare the real value of salary offers in two cities by taking into account differences in tax structures and the cost of living. In Table B.1, I use two cities I lived in as an example, with Montreal acting as the "home" city and Geneva as the "host," but you can easily substitute places relevant to your move. The following sections describe each of the items in the table. Because the main challenge is not making the calculation but rather collecting all the information, I indicate possible sources for each item. I used the metric system for the calculations since it is commonly used around the world and makes an easier basis for comparison.

Getting the Data

○ *Gross salary.* Usually your employer will give you this information in your contract. However, if you are trying to estimate before getting the details of your offer, especially as a new hire, you can consider looking at the salary data provided by the leading business school in the region you are heading to. Most business schools provide a detailed online report of the salaries their last year's graduates are earning and organize it by country and industry. For the purposes of this exercise, I used salary data from INSEAD 2003 placement reports *(www.insead.edu/mba/careers/full-timejobs.htm)* to estimate the income in Geneva (the data is for Switzerland in general), and 2003 employment statistics from McGill Management *(www.mcgill.ca/management/career/mba/stats)* to estimate the income in Montreal.

● *Taxes.* You should be able to get information on the tax structure from your employer, from your relocation consultant, or from your country's embassy or consulate in the host country. I found the Canadian and Swiss tax information online. In Canada, income tax is collected by both the federal government (20.5% on a salary of $80,000) and the provincial government (20% on the same). In Switzerland, income tax for foreigners is only collected by the Cantonal (regional) authorities, and it amounts to 22.3% on a salary of 140,000 CHF. While both countries automatically deduct unemployment and old age pension benefits from the paycheck (the rates are available online), it is important to note one major difference: Canadian taxes include health insurance, while in Switzerland this must be purchased from a private provider.

● *Other deductions.* These are everything you need to consider to arrive at a comparable Net Salary number. In this case, I included the amount I would have to spend on private health insurance in Switzerland, which is about 450 CHF/month with a 500 CHF annual deductible (for a person about 30 and in good health), or about 3.2 % of the gross salary. This is information you could get from a relocation consultant in Geneva or by searching Swiss insurance companies online.

● *Net salary.* Only after having considered taxes and all the separate deductions do you arrive at a Net Salary figure that is actually comparable. Still, this is not the end of your calculations. You must also take into account the difference in the cost of living in your home and host countries before you can actually know what will remain in your pocket at the end of the day.

● *Monthly lodging expenses.* This is easiest to find out during your Look-See trip as you visit potential apartments. However, it is also quite easy to find on the Internet by searching the classified ads in a local paper. The numbers I use in my chart are the approximate monthly rents for a one-bedroom apartment in downtown Montreal and Geneva, including heating but excluding utilities such as phone, cable TV, Internet, electricity, and gas.

● *Monthly living expenses at home.* When trying to establish your monthly living expenses at home, it is useful to look at a period of time, ideally six months or a year. That ensures that you account for things you would probably forget to consider when creating a budget, like the cost of repairing your computer or dry cleaning a spaghetti stain off your leather pants. By far the easiest way is to take your annual net income, adjust it for any increase or decrease in savings, and divide by 12. If this is not feasible, then you can try tracking your spending for at least three months. This can be a useful exercise to do anyway, as it can give you a breakdown of your spending. In my case, living in Montreal was approximately $1,300 CAD, excluding rent.

● *Cost of living factor.* This item translates your monthly expenses at home into a reasonable number abroad. Many relocation companies provide this kind of data to employers, at a fee, for use in designing expat compensation packages. Unfortunately, if you are a new hire trying to evaluate a local offer abroad, you are not likely to have access to this information, so you have to devise your own way of comparing the cost of living between your home and host countries. My approach involves three pillars. The first pillar is the famous *Big Mac index*, a comparison of the cost of a Big

Mac in countries across the world conducted by *The Economist* magazine. You can access the results online at *www.economist.com/ markets/Bigmac/Index.cfm*. Table B.2 uses data from the May 2004 issue of *The Economist*. According to this, the cost of living in Switzerland is 2.1 times the cost of living in Canada.

Table B.2 Comparing Costs of a Big Mac in Canada and Switzerland

BIG MAC	Canada	Switzerland
Cost in USD	$2.33	$4.90
Factor	1.0	2.1

Source: The Economist May 2004

○ The second pillar involves getting a sense for the cost of labor or services. A good measure is the cost of a five km taxi ride in your home and host countries, which is very easy to do verify during your Look-See Trip. As you can see in Table B.3, according to this measure the cost of living in Geneva is 2.4 times that in Montreal, which reflects the high cost of labor in Switzerland. This means that services like getting a haircut, getting a pair of pants hemmed by a seamstress, or hiring a technician to repair your washing machine will be very expensive.

○ The final pillar involves getting an idea of the cost of groceries, both local and imported, for a cross-section of food types. Again, you can easily collect this data by visiting a food store on your Look-See trip. As you can see in Table B.4, the cost of living in Geneva is only 1.8 times that in Montreal.

Table B.3 Comparing Taxi Rides in Montreal and Geneva

5 KM TAXI RIDE	MONTREAL (CAD)	GENEVA (CHF)
Starting fee on meter	2.75	6.30
Cost per kilometer	1.30	2.90
	9.25	20.80
	9.25	21.84
Factor	1.0	2.4

*1 CHF = 1.05 CAD

Table B.4 Comparing Costs of Groceries*

BASKET OF FOOD STAPLES	MONTREAL (CAD)	GENEVA (CHF)
1 liter of 2% milk	1.55	1.45
6 eggs	1.92	2.80
1 kg Kellogs Corn Flakes	8.60	13.47
1 kg ground beef	7.07	24.00
1 kg tomatoes	7.58	5.25
Total	26.72	46.97
Currency Conversion to CAD*	26.72	49.32
Factor	1.0	1.8

Source: http://magasin.iga.net/index_fr.html and www.migros-shop.ch
*1 CHF = 1.05 CAD

The final pillar involves getting an idea of the cost of groceries, both local and imported, for a cross-section of food types. Again, you can easily collect this data by visiting a food store on your Look-See trip. As you can see in Table B.4, the cost of living in Geneva is only 1.8 times that in Montreal.

Averaging the Big Mac, taxi, and grocery factors arrives at a cost-of-living factor in Geneva that is about 2.1 times that in Montreal.

○ *Estimated monthly living expenses abroad.* This means that my monthly expenses in Montreal of about $1,300 (1,235 CHF, after currency conversion) translate to an estimated monthly spending of 2,594 CHF in Switzerland.

○ *Annualized living expenses.* Multiply the monthly living expenses in Montreal and Geneva by 12 to arrive at the annual figures (15,600 CAD and 31,122 CHF, respectively).

○ *Total annualized expenses.* Add the annualized lodging expenses to the annualized living expenses in Montreal and Geneva to arrive at the total annualized expenses (25,200 CAD and 45,522 CHF).

○ *Net in pocket.* Subtract the total annualized expenses from the net salary numbers to figure out how much will be left in your pocket at the end of the day. In my example in Table B.1, I would-have 16,856 CAD left in Montreal and 50,325 CHF left in Geneva (52,840 CAD after currency conversion). Clearly, it is more advantageous from a financial perspective to live in Switzerland.

WEB RESOURCES

GenXpat. *www.genXpat.com.* The site to visit if you have any additional questions, wish to connect with other GenXpats, or book a "GenXpat" seminar for your company or academic institution.

The World Factbook. *www.cia.gov/cia/publications/factbook.* A great resource for basic country data such as demographics, economy, religion, and geography.

Expat Expert. *www.expatexpert.com.* Robin Pascoe's website, which has lots of articles on going abroad, living abroad, and coming home, written primarily with the traditional expat family in mind.

Expat Exchange. *www.expatexchange.com.* Provides a listing of suppliers for all expat needs (healthcare, finances, relocation, real estate, and so on) together with an online expat discussion and resource forum.

Expatica. *www.expatica.com.* A great European expat resource, including articles for an HR audience (in case you ever wonder what is going through your HR manager's mind) and a dating site.

Fons Trompenaars' website. *www.trompenaars.net/index1.html.* Offers a detailed description of his seven dimensions of culture.

Geert Hofstede's website. *www.geert-hofstede.com.* Offers a detailed description of his four cultural dimensions and shows how they apply to over fifty countries.

Intercultural Press. *www.interculturalpress.com.* Publisher of trade and professional books on living and working abroad and intercultural communication and theory.

Primacy Relocation. *www.primacy.com.* For your relocation needs.

The Global Citizen. *www.the-global-citizen.com.* A great starting point for an educational, volunteer, or part-time work experience abroad.

REFERENCEf

Bridges, William. 2003. *Managing Transitions: Making the Most of Change.* Cambridge, MA: Da Capo Press.

Hall, Edward T. 1981. *Beyond Culture.* Garden City, NJ: Anchor Press/Doubleday 1981.

Hess, Melissa Brayer, and Patricia Linderman. 2002. *The Expert Expatriate: Your Guide to Successful Relocation Abroad.* Yarmouth, ME: Intercultural Press.

Hofstede, Geert. 1997. *Cultures and Organizations: Software of the Mind.* Toronto, ON: McGraw-Hill Books.

Kruemplemann, Elizabeth. 2002. *The Global Citizen: A Guide to Creating an International Life and Career.* Berkeley, CA: Ten Speed Press.

Pascoe, Robin. 1998. *Culture Shock! Successful Living Abroad: A Wife's Guide.* Portland, OR: Graphic Arts Center Publishing Company.

Trompenaars, Fons, and Charles Hampden-Turner. 1998. *Riding the Waves of Culture: Understanding Diversity in Global Business* (2nd ed.) Toronto, ON: McGraw-Hill Books.

INDEX

T

tax structure/system in destination country, 32-33, 43, 200-01

third-world/first-world caveats, 16-17, 126-27, 144

time, attitude toward, 74, 90-91

tourism, 57

transferee, old vs. new assignment, priorities of, 60

Trompenaars, Fons, 83

V

values, cultural differences in, 18-19, 70, 71-73, 84-96

visas, residence/tourist, 34, 53, 170

W

White, Jennifer, 32, 36, 38, 169

work. *See* job demands/commitments

work environment, cultural differences in, 84-97

work permit, 34, 53, 170

work vs. recreation/social activities, 5, 55, 57-58, 119, 122, 161

working partner/accompanying partner. *See* accompanying
        partner

workplace, conflicts in, 85-86, 87-88, 89, 91, 92-93, 94-95, 96-97